No One Knows Their Names

Screenwriters In Hollywood

No One Knows Their Names
Screenwriters In Hollywood

Jorja Prover

Bowling Green State University Popular Press
Bowling Green, Ohio 43403

Copyright © 1994 by Bowling Green State University Popular Press

Library of Congress Catalog Card Number: 94-70377

ISBN: 0-87972-657-1 Clothbound
0-87972-658-X Paperback

Cover design by Anthony Manos

For Georgia Koulos Manos and Nicoletta Toyias Skrumbis

In loving memory

Acknowledgments

This project would not have been possible without the continuous support of Dr. Joseph Rosner. His contribution to this effort is impossible to describe. In addition, Lesbia Cordon, Anthony Manos and Robyn Manos offered invaluable help at various stages of this endeavor.

I am also grateful to Rosina Becerra, Robert B. Edgerton, Lewis L. Langness, Milton Miller, Manuel Miranda and Allen Johnson who each offered a thoughtful critique of an earlier version of this work in particular and the cross-cultural approach in general. Ms. Pat Browne and the entire staff of the Popular Press were extremely helpful in bringing the manuscript to publication.

Finally, the success of this project was dependent on a number of remarkable writers who gave generously of their time and trust. I am indebted to them for sharing their dreams. In turn, my debt to Stephen Prover is incalculable; he has helped make every dream come true.

Contents

Preface

✦ ✦ ✦

Where This Book Came From

This work began as a dissertation for a doctoral degree in anthropology. From the onset, many individuals—both inside and outside of the entertainment industry—questioned my motives. No one understood why an anthropologist would want to study Hollywood. Most people viewed anthropologists as intellectual eccentrics who witnessed initiation rites on South Sea islands or dug up skeletons of prehistoric humans. What was an anthropologist doing in Hollywood when everyone knew its most exotic rituals consisted of competing for desirable tables at local watering holes? There was nothing mysterious about Hollywood, everyone insisted. "You can't study what's happening here," a producer explained, "it's just a bunch of guys running around trying to make a deal."

I could not understand why so many chose to ignore the obvious: that entertainment is a multi-billion-dollar enterprise whose impact on everyday life cannot be overestimated. Because Hollywood has long affected behavior and beliefs, it offered fertile ground for an anthropologist eager to uncover the dynamics of mass culture. But skepticism about my purpose knew no limits. I was constantly asked if I was using this "anthropology story" as a ploy to break into the industry. From this I learned that when it came to getting ahead in Hollywood, anything was possible. Almost everything had been attempted—or at the very least—imagined.

It helped that I possessed no fantasies of "breaking into" Hollywood. I did not ask for any favors except the opportunity to watch and listen to what took place inside of people's offices and on production sets. Initially, I employed a standard ethnographic technique, using methods of participant observation and speaking with anyone remotely involved with the entertainment industry who would consent to an interview. As time went on, my contacts multiplied and I interviewed individuals with responsibility for creation and production. This first

1

phase of research consisted of interviews with 75 individuals working in Hollywood, including production assistants, producers, attorneys, agents, journalists, actors, "gofers," and secretaries.

I found myself intrigued by one particular group: writers working on feature films and television.[1] While many in the industry insisted that writers were essential to successful production, they also maintained that virtually anyone with a good idea could sell a script. Little reverence was expressed for the art or profession of screenwriting. I became interested in the object of this particular paradox—the writers who were seen as essential but unremarkable. They were both a culture unto themselves, worthy of further examination and a group that was potentially responsible for affecting mass American culture in myriad ways. I decided I wanted to understand this particular group—why and how they wrote and how they existed in the larger Hollywood structure.

I conducted ten in-depth interviews with screenwriters, concentrating on writers' work, values, past accomplishments, and future goals as well as their personal histories, concerns, and beliefs. On the basis of these pilot interviews, it became clear to me that writers could not be considered as one single, homogeneous group. I then expanded my research to include more majority writers and to add minority writers to the project.

This presented a new dilemma: how to determine just who constituted a minority group. Descriptive categories were established to guide both the gathering and analysis of data. A number of factors determined categories of writers. First, all information available concerning Guild membership was surveyed, including a list of minority committees obtained from the Guild. In addition, Guild statistics were reviewed. These revealed which minority categories the Guild used when collecting information on what they labeled "protected classes." Specific categories of minority writers were formulated using categories the Guild employed to indicate minority groups as well as minority writers' own designations. The following categories were established: 1) Majority writers; 2) African-American writers; 3) Latino writers; 4) Disabled writers; 5) Women writers. Individuals in each group were interviewed to explore issues identified during pilot research.

Rather than setting an arbitrary limit of individuals for sampling in each category, the number of writers interviewed was contingent on the quality of incoming information. If there was uniformity of responses among members of a particular category initially sampled, interviewing in that category was completed. Sampling within a group was terminated at the point of "theoretical saturation."[2] Conversely, certain categories were oversampled. Groups that traditionally have not received much attention were examined more extensively. In the cases of African-American and women writers, responses varied with a demonstrable lack of uniformity. After expanded sampling, this problem was resolved by formulating the "black female writer" category.

Depth interviews were conducted with writers in each category. One hundred and twelve individual writers in the entertainment industry were contacted. All 112 were interviewed informally, either over the telephone or in person to determine their status in Hollywood and their willingness to participate in further research. In the end, I conducted in-depth interviews with 55 television and screenwriters who gave generously of their time and related their experiences. Most contacts with writers were obtained through personal referrals. Although I requested assistance from the Writers Guild, the organization was extremely protective of its membership. They refused to release any information except members' names, recent credits, and the telephone numbers of writers' agents when available.[3]

These 55 formal interviews comprise the data for this research. Five majority writers and 15 minority writers were interviewed more than once to gather detailed data. In addition, I employed secondary sources, when useful, to augment interviews.

Subjects were obtained through personal reference. During initial research, phone calls made to writers randomly selected from the Writers Guild membership list elicited no response. By contrast, personal referrals resulted in interviews in all but one case. Additionally, a letter was sent, with Writers Guild cooperation, to all minority committees. Several individuals responded to the letter, including the leading members of each minority committee.

Subjects were interviewed for one to four hours. Each interview began with a statement of the study's purpose and an assurance of complete confidentiality. Unless there was an objection, all interviews were tape-recorded. Rather than standardized survey research, this project was designed as a qualitative examination of the elite of Hollywood writers. Because of this, an open-ended interview schedule, listing general categories and questions of interest, was employed (see Appendix). Interview topics emerged from pilot study interviews.

4 No One Knows Their Names

Depending on the subject's willingness and the course of the interview the same topics were covered in all interviews, although not necessarily in the same order, nor in the same depth.

After the process of data collection was completed, all material was subjected to an in-depth content analysis. The task of data analysis was approached with two separate goals. First, responses in each category of writer were analyzed. Similarities among category members led to a composite profile of writers within each group. Responses within each category were uniform with the exception of black female writers whose responses were not consistent with the black or female category, but were consistent as a separate group. As stated, a category of "black female writers" was constructed.

Once different groups of writers were described, then writers across categories were compared for significant similarities and differences in their responses. In addition, majority and minority writers were compared. While all writers shared certain experiences and problems, significant differences between groups emerged. These are noted with an interpretation of the implications of such differences.

The features characterizing Hollywood writers are described in this study. The dilemmas and patterns common to all writers are summarized. Following this, divergences are noted. The concerns different groups of writers confront while involved in the Hollywood production process are delineated.

These interviews provided a wealth of material, some of it surprising, all of it invaluable. The material was not edited to fit pre-conceived notions. Instead, findings flowed from these writers' accounts. The only alteration made involved writers' names. Pseudonyms are used throughout this book after 80 percent of writers interviewed indicated they would not speak for attribution.

To simply state that writers pen scripts for money or financial gain is to ignore many elements of this elite. Writers compose a stable group, aware of financial reward, but deriving their ideas and motivation from varied sources, at times totally removed from commercial considerations. The particular motives, beliefs, and impulses that Hollywood writers satisfy as part of participating in a multi-billion dollar industry are explored. Hollywood writers compose a diverse, angry, and articulate group. They deserve the attention—and respect—they have long been denied.

Notes

[1]It is necessary to clarify the meaning of the term "writer" in this study. In Hollywood, the term "screenwriter" is used specifically to denote an individual who writes treatments, scripts, and screenplays for feature length motion pictures that appear in theaters where the public pays admission. Correspondingly, the term "television writer" refers to an individual who writes treatments, scripts, and teleplays for episodic television, television movies, and mini-series, on either cable or network enterprises. There are various levels of expertise and individuals who pursue success in each area. For example, certain writers concentrate on episodic television, while others are mini-series "experts."

Many in Hollywood distinguish between television writers and feature length motion picture writers. Because whether a writer worked on feature films or television made no difference in their responses to interviews, for the purposes of this study, except when noted, the distinction will not be finely drawn. The terms "screenwriters," "television writers," and "writers" will all be used interchangeably to designate any individual who works within the entertainment industry in some capacity using writing skills. These individuals perform various functions: creating treatments from original ideas, working and collaborating on someone else's script with partners, adaptating a book, novel, or short story, or even "doctoring" another writer's work. Some also function as producers and, in rare cases, as directors. All individuals identified as writers have functioned as such during their careers.

[2]Glaser and Strauss 1967: 61.

[3]This data was published in the *Writers Guild Directory*, a listing available to the public for a small fee.

Chapter One

✦ ✦ ✦

Why Another Book about Hollywood Writers?

> When people in Los Angeles talk about "this town," they do not mean Los Angeles, nor do they exactly mean what many of them call "the community"... "This town" is broader, and means just "the industry," which, tellingly, is the way people who make television and motion pictures refer to the environment in which they work. The extent to which the industry in question resembles conventional industries is often obscured by its unconventional product, which requires that its "workers" perform in unconventional ways, for which they are paid unconventional sums of money: some people do make big money writing and directing and producing and acting in television, and some people also make big money, although considerably less big, writing and directing and producing and acting in motion pictures. (Didion 158)

Hollywood represents a cynosure of modern life.[1] The entertainment industry has long captivated the American public, offering artistry, new technology, and an escape from reality. In addition, Hollywood has come to embody the ethos of overnight success, fostering the worldview that with luck and ambition, virtually anyone can break into the business and find prosperity and adulation. Finally, Hollywood has invented the celebrity elite—composed of individuals elevated to a status approaching that of royalty.

In representing the royalty of American culture—evoking images of wealth, power and prestige—the elite offer fantasy existences for the vicarious experience of their public, perpetuating the fascination with Hollywood. A favorite joke in Hollywood refers to the two types of people in America: people who are star struck and people who lie and say they are not.

Because of this interest, an extensive and varied literature on the entertainment industry has developed. Generally books about Hollywood

7

can be characterized as one of five major "types," although there is considerable overlap between categories. First, there are the numerous reference books containing facts and statistics on virtually every aspect of the industry: directories, encyclopedias, and filmographies. Many are updated on a yearly basis such as *The Hollywood Reporter Blue Book* which offers a guide to everything from production companies to "hotels, restaurants and leisure time activities." This category also includes encyclopedic accounts on the order of Leslie Halliwell's *Filmgoer's Companion, The Oxford Companion to Film* as well as the complete, if tedious, U.S. Government Printing Office *Catalog of Copyright Entries.*

Second is the group of books on the history of film and television, which includes general histories of the entertainment industry as well as accounts of specific events, such as the establishment of the Writers Guild and the subsequent blacklisting of members of the Hollywood community. Neil Gabler's *An Empire of Their Own: How the Jews Invented Hollywood* represents a noteworthy recent effort in this area. His work details the lives and maneuverings of the moguls who established the entertainment industry, creating, as Gabler terms it,

a "shadow" America, one which idealized every old glorifying bromide about the country...a powerful cluster of ideas and images—so powerful that, in a sense, they colonized the American imagination. No one could think about this country without thinking about the movies. (6-7)

This second major category also encompasses journalistic exposés, focusing on particularly sensational stories in industry history. The early 1980s brought *Indecent Exposure*, David McClintick's exposé of the David Begelman scandal at Columbia Pictures. This work was followed by Steven Bach's *Final Cut*, an in-depth account of how Michael Cimino's financial excesses during the production of the critical and commercial flop *Heaven's Gate* destroyed United Artists Pictures. Steve Wick's work *Bad Company* chronicled the collision of ambition, drugs, and murder during the production of the feature film *The Cotton Club*. Finally, Ron Brownstein's work *The Power and the Glory* attempted to draw connections between Hollywood and Washington, D.C.— describing how political power and industry glamour have fed off each other in the exercise of the American political process.

A third category consists of books that can be classified as either biographical or career studies of major Hollywood figures. These include the celebrity autobiographies that reach bestseller status— exemplified by such recent works as *Moving Pictures* by Ali MacGraw and *What's It All About?* by Michael Caine.[2] Equal in popularity to celebrity autobiographies are biographies, usually written about actors, analyzing their performances and personal lives with equal fervor (Kelley; Bragg). More recently, however, A. Scott Berg's work *Goldwyn* constituted both a scholarly effort and a commercial success, a well-researched view of the mogul who invented his name and his identity along with the films once described as having the "Goldwyn" touch. Similar to Berg's, was David Thomson's book on mogul David O. Selznick. Along with these traditional works, there are the less sanitized, more irreverent accounts of life in the industry written by William Goldman and Larry McMurtry.

The fourth category consists of books aimed at analysis of entertainment content from a specific perspective whether offering film reviews or exposition on a particular film or film genre. Collections of reviews by television and film critics abound. Pauline Kael, Roger Ebert, Richard Schickel, and Leonard Maltin are print and media critics who have collected and published their articles and observations. Other film critics have written sensitive analyses of film content including Mollie Haskell's feminist appraisals and Ethan Mordden's historical overviews. Currently, *Sneak Previews* critic Michael Medved has drawn attention and ire in response to his work, *Hollywood vs. America: Popular Culture and the War Against Traditional Values,* which offers part movie review and part social polemic.

Finally, the fifth, and possibly most confused category, encompasses those books that attempt to scrutinize the internal dynamics of the entertainment industry. Some, such as Linda Stuart's work, *Getting Your Script Through the Hollywood Maze,* offer straightforward advice on how to "break into" the entertainment industry.

More importantly, this category also includes the rare but ambitious efforts at understanding the actual internal workings of Hollywood. The oldest survey, Hortense Powdermaker's *Hollywood: The Dream Factory,* is still cited because this area remains neglected.[3] Finally, in 1986, Mark Litwak updated Powdermaker, offering an overview of the dynamics of power and influence in what he terms the "new Hollywood." Both books, while earnest efforts, suffer from the generality of their approaches. In covering several aspects of the industry, they fail to find a focus and animate life in Hollywood in any particular depth.

Certain authors have focused on the creative process behind a single project. For example, in 1983, Susan Dworkin described the production of *Tootsie*, revealing the sexist behavior of producer-director, Sydney Pollak and star Dustin Hoffman, despite the proclaimed feminist theme of the film. More recently, Julie Salomon's 1991 work, *The Devil's Candy*, offered a firsthand account of the creative confusion behind the filming of the bestseller turned box office bomb *The Bonfire of the Vanities*.[4]

Rather than concentrate on a particular project, John Gregory Dunne, a novelist, journalist and screenwriter, studied a specific locale: the movie studio. Dunne provided an insider's view of industry organization after being permitted unlimited access to 20th Century Fox Studios for one year, permission Richard Zanuck was later criticized for granting. Dunne reported what he saw and heard, a straightforward record of filmmaking and studio politics. Although over 20 years old, Dunne's work has yet to be improved upon.

The actual mechanics of industry life remain largely unexplored. In addition, despite the books composing each of these five categories, the motives driving the people who work in Hollywood remained misunderstood. It is unclear what needs these individuals may be trying to meet as they produce entertainment. Are they "culture-makers," sending a message to the global village[5] or are they money-makers, blind to cultural concerns?[6]

Little has been written on actual development of entertainment. Just what dynamics are at work in the creation of the powerful financial and social product of television and film? Despite the public fascination with "the industry," what is written about Hollywood rarely focuses on understanding the internal dynamics and personalities responsible for the operation of this "dream-making" machine.

One particular group whose work is fundamental to the machinery of Hollywood is its writers. These writers reside in an occupational purgatory somewhere between celebrity and anonymity. They possess neither recognizable names nor faces, yet they compose an elite, playing an integral role in the Hollywood structure, indirectly influencing American and international culture. Although their work is rarely preserved intact, they are the originators of plots, characters, and themes that will endure in one form or another until public screening. Richard Corliss contends that writers as well as directors are "auteurs." And no less than Orson Wells offered his opinion that "...the writer should have the first and last word in filmmaking, the only better alternative being the writer-director, but the stress on the first word" (Corliss xxii).

Brady lists three reasons why writers are powerful forces in Hollywood. First, current filmmakers (Spielberg, Lucas, Coppola, Scorcese) are the products of film schools where writing is valued. Second, with the cost of filmmaking escalating, all factors involved in the process are considered carefully. The financial commitment for "average films" ranges from $35 to $40 million. Consequently, script quality gains significance with such a costly investment. Studio executives, investors, and producers are aware that famous names and large budgets do not insure a film's success.[7] Third, with structural changes in Hollywood, the *creative* impact of the studio executive or producer has diminished. Today, producers and studios concentrate on the financing and distribution of films. The new movie "moguls" function more as attorneys and accountants than artists. The creative responsibility rests with writers and directors. According to George Lucas:

You can put us on a leash, keep us under control. But we are the guys who dig out the gold. The man in the executive tower cannot do that. The studios are corporations and the men who run them are bureaucrats...They go to parties and they hire people who know people. But the power lies with us—the ones who actually know how to make movies. (Brady 25)

The importance of writers to entertainment production emerged as a constant theme in my early research. During ethnographic work in Hollywood, I was repeatedly told that the key to successful entertainment was effective writing; without it, a project would languish and never reach production. But while people working within the industry emphasized the importance of writing, the same individuals added a contradictory claim: that screenwriting was relatively simple, requiring little unusual skill or ability.

This paradox illustrates the status of the Hollywood writer. Within the structure of Hollywood, writers are essential but undervalued. This problem of diminished value is reinforced by their virtual invisibility to the general public.

12 No One Knows Their Names

Indeed, this invisibility is the hallmark of Hollywood writers; it is the source of both their security and their despair. Writers are seldom blamed for a flop. But audiences do not clamor to see a film or select a television program on the basis of who wrote the script. Because they are invisible and often indistinguishable from each other, their commercial and artistic achievements and failures are often overlooked or attributed to someone else. This invisibility persists, despite the efforts of several writers at accurately portraying their contribution to the entertainment industry in articles and memoirs such as Benjamin Stein's *Diary of a Mad Screenwriter*, romans à clef like Michael Tolkin's *The Player* and Peter Viertel's *White Hunter, Black Heart*, and novels such as *The Return of Mr. Hollywood* by Josh Greenfeld, *The Deal* by Peter Lefcourt, and Bruce Wagner's *Force Majeure*. Probably most well known is William Goldman's irreverent self-portrait, *Adventures in the Screen Trade*, whose cynical proviso that in Hollywood "nobody knows anything" is constantly repeated by other habitues of the industry.[8] While writers have tried to set matters straight—and perhaps enhance their incomes—the recognition they desire has eluded them. Audiences simply do not care. This lack of public interest in screenwriters is matched only by the utter lack of regard for writers within the industry itself.

It is this lack of regard or respect within the industry, even more than their identity of invisibility, that plagues Hollywood writers. Journalist David Thomson cynically explained:

No writer in Hollywood has much enjoyed the position; it is a little too much on its knees with its bare ass in the cool air, waiting. A writer is like a divorce lawyer or a private eye: when you want them you have to have them; but later you despise them. If you're the writer, you feel privileged, invited up to the big house, flattered, confided in, given money and the private number, hungered after even, because you can solve the problem. So you solve it, you write it away and people laugh and say, Why there wasn't really a problem was there? Just see yourself out, and count your money outside, not here. You end up humiliated and demoralized and that's why they call you again. (Thomson, "Trouble" 59)

Writers are more than invisible—they do not count. Most writers working today exert little clout in the industry, unable to control what happens to their work. It is true that many writers are paid handsomely to suffer such indignities. A successful screenwriter can command a yearly income in excess of $1 million.[9] While, in William Goldman's words, "Hollywood overpays for silence," money can only partially ease writers' frustration at their powerlessness. Their lack of control naturally engenders feelings of exploitation and pessimism. In the early 1930s, screenwriter Lester Cole claimed that Hollywood executives viewed writers as "the niggers of the studio system" (Schwartz 12). Little has changed when 50 years later Robert Towne contends, "I think that writers have tended to be the niggers of the industry, so to speak."

In reality, these individuals are not "niggers," they are not even black. Writers Guild statistics reveal that the majority of Hollywood writers are white, male, and according to conventional wisdom—Jewish.[10] It is ironic that these "majority" writers employ a racial stereotype to dramatize their plight in Hollywood. For the actual "underrepresented" writers—African-Americans, women, the disabled, and ethnic minorities—things are even more complicated. Invisibility and exploitation are merely part of the problem. In describing their experiences in the industry many minority writers have accused the Hollywood establishment of practicing something more insidious: discrimination. While one black woman quipped, "To be a writer you've got to be short and Jewish," conviction lurked behind her joke. During interviews, many ethnic minority writers claimed that Hollywood was closed to them, their professional opportunities limited because they were "different."

This book considers Hollywood writers as a group. It is neither a collection of profiles on the "superstars" of screenwriting, an affectionate retrospective, nor a guide on how to sell a script. Instead, this work looks at some of the joys and frustrations experienced by writers working in Hollywood today. Their personal and professional histories illustrate how writers identify themselves and how they are stratified within the industry. Additionally each writer's goals, disappointments, and accomplishments illuminate the struggle between personal integrity and professional aspiration.

Their creative struggles and political in-fights are revealed, frequently in writers' own words. These individuals describe the experience of working in isolation, trying to piece together a plot or rewrite lines of dialogue they believed were "perfect." They also discuss the process of pitching ideas to producers and standing by, passively watching what happens to their work once it is sold. They discuss their anger and their coming to terms with the "industry."

In discussing their own conflicts these writers also reveal a great deal about the politics of Hollywood—who gets to write and why. This opens a second area for investigation. In addition to studying the individual sensibilities of the screenwriter, this book explores the experience of minority writers who work with the dual purpose of gaining acceptance and bringing different cultural views to Hollywood. There are several reasons minority writers, including women, African-Americans, Latinos, and the disabled, merit a specific consideration. First, and perhaps most obviously, this is an overlooked population. To the extent that motion picture and television writers have been overlooked, the minority writer has not even been mentioned. The prototypical white Jewish male writer has been the focus of the limited work on Hollywood writers.[11] Second, minorities constitute more recently arrived groups in Hollywood. Their emergence and impact on the entertainment industry demonstrates how Hollywood responds to changes in its profile that mirror changes in the makeup of American society. Third, the position of minority groups within an elite can be explored and their subcultural impact can be assessed. The face of Hollywood *may* be changing as part of the growing visibility of minorities. However, this is a hazardous assumption. The actual position and power of underrepresented groups in the entertainment industry must be determined to better comprehend just who is generating the American public's dreams.

Both majority and minority writers are analyzed in terms of their awareness of cultural trends, values, and themes in their work. In addition, the impact of personal beliefs and behavior patterns on screenwriting is assessed. This book considers the cultural backgrounds of Hollywood writers and evaluates whether differences in background affect the writer's work—both creatively and in the industry structure. There will be specific attention to the particular dilemmas minority group writers face in Hollywood.

In addition, the reaction of these writers to the breakthroughs achieved by women such as Callie Khouri and Linda Bloodworth-Thomason along with African-Americans such as Spike Lee and Bill Cosby will be examined.

In short, this is the story of screenwriters: a group essential to the dream-making machinery of Hollywood, a group that conceivably, albeit indirectly, influences American culture. This book represents an effort at stepping inside the reality of the Hollywood writer and understanding the phenomenology of the industry from their perspective.

Notes

[1]The words "Hollywood," "entertainment industry," "film industry" and "motion picture industry" (among others) will be used interchangeably to connote the enterprise involved in the creation and manufacture of filmed entertainment for mass consumption. No distinction is made between motion pictures and television.

[2]These range from the biographical and autobiographical (Ross and Ross 1961; Behlmer 1972; Huston 1980; Bergen 1984) to the more general reminiscences (Bogdanovich 1973; Schulberg 1981; Viertel 1992) and even rather grisly gossip compilations (Anger 1975, 1983).

[3]See Mark Litwak in *Reel Power*. He cites Powdermaker as recently as 1986.

[4]Dworkin (1984) also observed and interviewed Brian DePalma, a director noted for films with excessive violence. Both of Dworkin's works describe what creators consider as they manufacture entertainment.

[5]Entertainment has been viewed as an effective vehicle to potentially impact social behavior in more positive ways. The late multi-millionaire philanthropist Armand Hammer contacted Bill Cosby, requesting the opportunity to appear as a character on his television series. According to Hammer, such an appearance would enable him to "send a message" to the American public, encouraging them to contribute money and personal effort to help cure cancer. Hammer claimed that television was the single most effective means of reaching the public. Cosby commissioned a special script in which Hammer plays a grandfather watching his grandson dying of a brain tumor. Hammer's character subsequently exhorts Cosby's alter-ego, Dr. Clifford Huxtable to "do something—write your congressman," even offering him a pen and paper.

[6]First and foremost, is the issue of revenue. Total theater admissions at U.S. theaters in 1992 numbered 3,040,000,000. In 1992, the industry earned over $6 billion. Today, the average motion picture budget ranges between $35 and $40 million, although in an extreme cases, such as James Cameron's *The Abyss,* spending can exceed $60 million. The motion picture industry is a major economic and cultural enterprise. It is estimated that throughout the 1990s, motion pictures will attract approximately three to five billion viewers to theaters each year, generating annual revenues in excess of $8 billion.

On a larger scale, Hollywood's impact can be felt on patterns of consumer spending. The popularity of men's undershirts fell and rose respectively with a

16   No One Knows Their Names

bare-chested Clark Gable of *It Happened One Night* being replaced as a role model by Marlon Brando in his torn undershirt in *A Streetcar Named Desire* (Cook 1981). More recently, the Mars Candy Company expressed their regret at failing to negotiate an agreement with Steven Spielberg for their candies to appear in *E.T.* Instead, the alien consumed the chocolate candies of their rival: Reese's. Mars estimates the lost opportunity may have cost their company revenues in the millions. Goldman (1983) has detailed the shrewdness of advertisers and corporations who help finance a motion picture if their product is prominently displayed somewhere in the plot, no matter how irrelevant its appearance. Filmmakers frequently orchestrate film openings with the introduction of new products to the American market, hoping for maximum impact on consumer spending. George Lucas is considered a master of this technique, with revenues in the hundreds of millions proving the wisdom of his marketing strategy (Blumenthal 1984).

[7]The presence of "name" actors does not insure box office success. In the past, *She-Devil* starring Meryl Streep and Roseanne Barr and *The Two Jakes* directed by and starring Jack Nicholson both failed to draw audiences. Most recently, *Godfather III* did not live up to Paramount's profit expectations.

[8]See, for example, Bach in *Final Cut* (1985) and Litwak in *Reel Power* (1986).

[9]In the wake of the success of *Basic Instinct*, screenwriter Joe Eszterhas is reportedly paid $5 million per screenplay.

[10]This prototype represents the majority of Hollywood writers, in sheer numbers as well as success. Statistically speaking, 79.8 percent of the Writers Guild 6000+ membership consists of white males (WGAW 1986).

[11]In fact, the prototypical Hollywood writer is a Caucasian male between the ages of 30 and 60, and the most well-known among them are predominantly Jewish. These demographics repeatedly surface in the literature of Hollywood. John Brady's book, *The Craft of the Screenwriter* (1981) consists of interviews with six individuals labeled among the "most successful" writers who have worked in Hollywood. All six writers were male and white, and five out of the six were Jewish. Richard Corliss in *Talking Pictures: Screenwriters in American Cinema* (1974) examines the work of 39 American "author-auteurs." Of these, two are female co-authors (one, Ruth Gordon has her name enclosed in parentheses as a co-author with her husband Garson Kanin), the remaining 37 are males. With the exception of three women (Lillian Hellman, Anita Loos and Dorothy Parker), Ian Hamilton's *Writers in Hollywood* is a historical account of white male writers as well. Clearly, Hollywood writers have been portrayed as a homogeneous group, and literature reflects reality.

Chapter Two

✦ ✦ ✦

Hollywood Writers:
Cases in Point

"The typical screenwriter is an intelligent New York Jewish kid whose mother thought every word he had to say was brilliant." This observation, from a veteran Hollywood journalist, characterizes the most highly visible individuals working as writers in the entertainment industry. In fact, Hollywood writers are articulate, urban, and many—although not all—are Jewish. Their similarities extend beyond this simple description. These writers grew up in largely middle-class households where they absorbed the traditional values of education, hard work, and upward mobility. As adults they lead rather conventional lives, complete with spouses, children, and mortgages. While unexceptional, many find their existence is not untroubled. During interviews, several writers discussed emotional struggles and were candid about seeking psychotherapy.[1]

Along with these similarities, there are surprising differences. Several younger writers I spoke with had invested years in graduate education, acquiring advanced degrees in English or Theater Arts. Others maintained careers in white-collar professions writing "on the side." Some earn incomes in seven figures while others have accomplished little since selling their first property. One writer recalled a past life in medieval England, while another planned a future "anywhere but Hollywood." The disparity in their thoughts undercut the apparent uniformity of their existences.

Many writers are settled in the beaches, canyons and hillsides of Los Angeles. Certain enclaves attract different groups. Many gay writers settle in West Hollywood, while successful white male writers and their families populate residential Brentwood and Santa Monica. Sometimes, homes are rented rather than owned, without pools or tennis courts. Still,

17

several writers live alongside the famous and powerful in Hollywood, sharing more than geography. They frequent the same restaurants, enroll their children in the same schools, and vacation in the same resorts. "You've got to get this straight," one writer remarked, "We're like people working for the brewers in Milwaukee. Hollywood is just the company town."

If this statement is accurate, Hollywood is a company town in the extreme. The "industry" in this company town attracts international attention and the writer labors in what Powdermaker once termed the "dream factory." Using pseudonyms, what follows are brief portraits of several different screenwriters, a random selection among the individuals interviewed.

Ian Singer is the quintessential Hollywood screenwriter: white, male and Jewish. He smokes large cigars, wears Nike running shoes, and holds court in a plush office on a major studio lot where he twits his visitors with an endless stream of obscenities and Yiddish. There are limos and dinners at Spago and $1 million a year guaranteed before he writes one word. No one knows his name and he could care less. The fact of the matter is, Singer has what every writer wants: control. Whether power is measured in lines of credit or in the ability to produce one's own projects, Singer has plenty of everything. But it wasn't always this easy.

He survived Hollywood for 15 years, a television hack who achieved the moderate success required to support a house in the flats of Beverly Hills, an ex-wife, a housekeeper, and three cats in the backyard. There was never enough for a foreign luxury car or a Bel-Air address, but Singer made his living as a journeyman writer—one of many—who existed on the outskirts of the industry elite.

The change in his career status came with a thankless writing assignment. A major television network was attempting to produce a mini-series from a best-selling novel. The mercurial author of the novel was interfering with the television adaptation. According to the novelist, none of the scripts met with his approval, no one was quite good enough to adapt the novel, and three writers had already quit in frustration.

In desperation, the network turned to Singer, giving him one weekend to come up with a treatment. Singer's method was simple. He sat down, read through the 1000-plus-page opus once, turned to the opening page and read through again. Monday morning he possessed a treatment and a contract. With the novelist assuaged, the mini-series proceeded to become a ratings success and Singer had gone from a hack to a man who could "name his price." He attended the Emmy Awards ceremony that year in tuxedo, Nikes, and cigar. Shortly after that, he received a Porsche as a "gift" from a grateful network executive along with the keys to the suite on the studio lot.

Frank Gotham also fits the prototype of the Hollywood screenwriter. He is a white and male and while he is not Jewish, he is verbal, urbane, and dedicated to the industry.

Frank Gotham had always wanted to make movies: full-length feature films with provocative themes, stellar casts, and worldwide distribution. Frank suspected there were others like him, although he remained purposely unaware of the extent of the competition. He felt he would be the one to make it.

For seven years at University of Southern California, he had worked halfheartedly on his Ph.D. in Social Psychology knowing, all along, he would never end up an academician. But graduate school held a hidden attraction. As part of his research Frank made documentary films. Sometimes the "films" turned out resembling nothing so much as a home movie. But he began to learn—mainly through the mistakes he made—about how a film was put together. There was something even more fundamental than the technical wrongs and rights. No matter where the movie ended up, it always began with the idea and the words that structured what would happen, or not happen, on-screen. Sometimes the plan was ignored and the film took on a life of its own. Things turned out directly the opposite of what was written down. But in most cases, the screenplay was where everything began. Frank Gotham learned that if he wanted to make movies, he would have to write.

Armed with several "how-to" manuals, Frank went to work on his first screenplay. He wrote about what he knew (the books advised that) and his idea was certainly unusual. The screenplay was about an elderly woman, Bette, and her community of friends among the homeless in downtown Los Angeles. Based on Frank's own experiences studying the homeless, it was a lovely script, full of memorable characters and narrative surprise. All that remained was the problem of how to sell it. Frank had neither an agent nor connections. There was no one he could pitch the idea to—he was not even sure *how* to pitch an idea. Unsure of himself, he entered the USC screenwriting competition. Then the worst happened. He won.

The morning after the award was announced, the development department at Universal Studios offered him $30,000 for a one-year option on the screenplay. A man named Dana Powell from the William Morris agency called up and asked Frank to mail over his latest project so they could talk about the possibility of "representation." Frank was convinced he was on his way. He joined the Writers Guild, took a leave of absence from school, moved to the beach and began to write full time. The money would last him six months, he figured, and by then he would have sold his next screenplay.

Three years later Frank returned to USC, and work on his Ph.D. Universal had decided to drop their option after one year and no one else had been interested in his screenplay. Dana Powell no longer returned his calls. There were new screenplays and other ideas but no one in Hollywood was very interested in Frank.

There are other individuals, both successful and struggling, with experiences similar to those of Ian Singer and Frank Gotham. These writers differ only because they are members of the differing under-represented groups that compose the small and yet often vocally disgruntled factions within the Hollywood screenwriters elite.

Linda Spencer is an African-American woman in her late thirties full of energy and ambition. She lives in the hills of Alta-Dena in an upscale neighborhood. But the house is rented and the pool has not been cleaned since she arrived. Still, there is a charisma and openhandedness about her that is disarming. Visitors to her home are fed lentil soup and information with equal abandon.

As a black woman, Spencer is a double minority, and she feels her protected class status keenly. She recites a laundry list of incidents involving dashed hopes and discrimination, offering compliments and indictments while recounting what happened. Her stories involve heroes—like Calvin Kelley and Wanda Coleman—and villains—who include some of the powerful of Hollywood. But even here, choosing sides, Spencer makes mistakes. She readily identifies herself with those who—while politically active—have not acquired adequate connections inside the industry. Those who shout the loudest frequently, it seems, produce the least. And without any substantial writing credits, they stand a good chance of losing their membership in the Guild as well.

Spencer grew up in Washington, D.C., and her initial professional credentials were impeccable. She worked and wrote for National Public Radio and then, curious about Hollywood, made her way west with absolutely no contacts and a child to support. Her energy and drive, she was certain, would be enough to insure her success. Once on the west coast, she applied and was admitted to the American Film Institute, where she received a minority scholarship and made a television appearance as one of the future generation of Hollywood filmmakers. Described as "one of the shining lights in the future of Hollywood," Spencer felt her faith in herself had been justified. Then, problems began.

Before her second year at AFI, the scholarship was inexplicably withdrawn. "Discontinued" was the only explanation she received. Worse than this blow, however, was her experience at the hands of producers in the industry. Repeatedly promised jobs, she followed "great" opportunities that led nowhere. At first she lived off of savings until she was forced to seek work far from the confines of the entertainment industry. She worked as a temporary secretary in several law firms. In all this time, she remained hopeful about her ability to break into the industry. There were letters sent off to mailing lists of 100 people and dubious contacts made. Spencer began the cycle of phone calls and interviews several times, but failed to secure a position.

At the same time, Spencer grew politically active in the Writers Guild. She participated in meetings of the Black Writers committee, attending strategy sessions that lasted long into the night, with statistics collected and protests lodged. The creative process was replaced by the political process and Spencer's experience of Hollywood became an account of black protests with conversations from meetings repeated verbatim. She was so busy arguing and protesting and cataloging inequities, she barely had time to work on a sample script. And in the end, despite all the activism, her experience was marked with despair. The night a WGA statistical study on minorities in Hollywood was read, she felt utterly bereft of hope for the future and saddened she had so little to show for so much effort.

Finally, emotionally and physically exhausted, Spencer fled on a two-week tour to Europe. The trip organization was cheap and seedy and she abandoned the group after two days. Stranded in Rome, she miraculously talked her way into a job at an Italian studio. In Italy she found acceptance and an atmosphere free of the discrimination typical of the American film industry. Eventually she sought and received money for her own independent production and she successfully wrote and directed a feature film in Italy. Now she was back in the United States, looking for an American distributor. She told me the film was being cut and extended an invitation to the screening. I never heard about the work again.

While Linda Spencer's minority status in Hollywood gave rise to political activism, there are other minority writers who rarely contemplate their status as members of a "protected class." This lack of minority identity was evinced by Reuben Contla, a Latino who had grown up in East Los Angeles but labeled himself a "screenwriter, period."

I met Reuben Contla in his home, the former mansion of a movie star located in the Hollywood hills. He was spending a last month in the house, before a bank foreclosed on the mortgage. The walls of the house were papered with magazine articles detailing Contla's glory days in Hollywood. Contla did not behave like a man facing eviction, laughing when he explained that while money was tight for the time being, the problem was temporary. Enthusiastically, he outlined his next project, a feature film. He was very close to selling the screenplay to an up and coming Hispanic actor who would help produce and star in the film.

Contla appeared to be an updated version of Sammy Glick, the infamous protagonist of Budd Schulberg's novel *What Makes Sammy Run?* He was fast-talking, glib, and convincing. His study, which occupied the bottom floor of the mansion, was crammed with papers and scripts. A bulletin board behind his desk, full of index cards, detailed the progression of scenes in his latest project. The phone rang non-stop and in between taking calls Contla offered an oral history of his life as a screenwriter. After graduating from California State University, Los Angeles, he secured an appointment at Universal Studios through the proverbial "friend of a friend," pitched and sold a story idea for a weekly situation comedy. He parlayed this success into a television scriptwriting assignment and was eventually hired as a staff writer for another weekly situation comedy. His own background had not impeded his progress. There was no problem, he insisted, in a boy from East Los Angeles writing a sitcom about the ups and downs of white middle-class Americans.

The job paid handsomely—both financially and in providing an insider education. Contla learned about the industry, receiving an on-the-job tutorial in the mechanics of scriptwriting. He also made professional and personal contacts in the Hollywood structure, lining up potential deals and pursuing a romance with one of the co-stars of the situation comedy. When his photograph appeared on the front page of the *National Enquirer* and the back page of *The Hollywood Reporter*, Contla was convinced he had arrived.

Increasingly confident after his early success, Contla decided to make a break. While staff work on a Top 10 sitcom was a secure situation and exciting in its way, he felt the pull of feature films and decided to go out on his own as a freelance writer. His good luck held. Shortly after Contla declared his independence, the sitcom was cancelled. If he was indeed prescient, the future appeared promising. A producer expressed interest in one of his scripts: a screenplay about a subject he suddenly claimed to know intimately—gang life in East L.A.—but in the midst of rewrites he was abruptly told the project was dead: "There was too much violence in L.A. Gangs were out, high-tech was in."

Selling other ideas was not as easy. Contla began to suspect that the cliches were accurate: feature film production was an altogether different enterprise, nothing like working for network television. Frustrated and beginning to worry about his finances, Contla pitched an idea for a mini-series to network television executives. Even back in his more familiar surroundings, little interest was expressed in his concept. His girlfriend broke up with him, there was no steady paycheck, and his mortgage payments were not being made.

In the midst of this, Contla maintained his equilibrium and his sense of humor. He did not feel discriminated against because he was Latino. He blamed it on "bad luck, bad timing" and other assorted accidents of fate. He remained enthusiastic about his latest project, a screenplay for a film he was collaborating on with his new partner, the grandson of a famous Hollywood mogul. "It doesn't hurt to have that last name on the screenplay," Contla grinned, "I'm gonna sell the damn thing one way or another. I'm a survivor."

Ellen Marcus also describes herself as a survivor. Drinking coffee in the kitchen of her home in Rustic Canyon, she looks like the wife of an affluent professional—which she once was—comfortable with her European appliances and fashionably worn wicker furniture. In reality, she is a divorcee who raised four children and succeeded as a screenwriter after an unwanted divorce. Marcus is passionate about her writing and about the creative process, convinced that it engenders the type of self-exploration crucial to insuring personal as well as professional growth.

There was no film school in Ellen Marcus's background, although she possesses a Hollywood pedigree of sorts. Choosing her words carefully, she recalled her upbringing as the child of two highly successful Hollywood screenwriters. Physically and psychologically abused, memories and emotional scars have caused her to regard both her mother and father—and by extension Hollywood—somewhat warily. She had always kept her distance from the industry. But with her divorce papers signed and her finances unsettled, she enrolled in a UCLA extension course and learned the fundamentals of screenwriting, determined to earn a living in Hollywood.

Using contacts made through her family and the writing she worked on zealously, Marcus began to sell her material. She earned screen writing awards and lucrative contracts for Top 10 television shows and mini-series. But along with success came the issue of professional identity. Marcus knew she was not "one of the boys," as the sexual overtures she received from more than one producer soon proved. Rejection brought severe consequences, as she discovered when she found herself out of a job after resisting the advances of one powerful producer. But she has never lost sight of who she is—a minority, a woman in Hollywood—whose credentials can be lifted at any time.

Ellen Marcus claimed she was always aware of her status as an outsider in Hollywood. Such insight does not come as readily to other writers. Robert Walters is tall, lanky, and looks as if he has spent a lifetime in professional athletics. He speaks in a deep baritone, a holdover from his days working as a Shakespearian actor in Britain. Although he identifies himself as a black screenwriter and has been politically involved, his past history is checkered and he names novelist Harold Robbins as a mentor.

Walters is an intriguing combination of creative fire and political savvy. Ideas for projects shoot from his mouth in staccato bursts. In the same sentence he describes a screenplay about white hunters in Kenya and a proposed television series about ghetto kids in Watts. Along with describing specific projects, he insists he is concerned with "making things better," influencing the audience using film and television.

Walters's story did not match that of other screenwriters, he did not arrive in Hollywood with a "dream." He gravitated to the industry by default, after pursuing interests in the music business and an acting career. By the time he reached Hollywood, he had few illusions, but a great deal of ambition. Harold Robbins took an interest in Walters while he was still struggling to find work as an actor. Robbins suggested he try writing instead and introduced him to several established writers. These introductions provided an important connection that led to a professional union with the unthinkable: a white male writer, David Lennox. The partnership prospered with both writers hotly in demand for television work during the 1980s. Walters's record reads as a list of some of the most successful and innovative shows to grace the small screen. With a body of impressive work behind him, Walters grew anxious to try writing alone. In 1990, the collaborators parted amicably and Walters began accepting solo assignments. The work was steady and initially Walters was thrilled with the demands for his service. He was even forced to reject offers because of limits on his time. Walters was so busy he ignored what was happening to him until two years had passed. During a meeting with studio executives, he realized he was writing exclusively for black shows. There was an up side. He was intensely involved in the creation and production of several landmark projects. And financially he was a success. But at the end of ten years of writing in Hollywood, he was not moving ahead. And he was afraid.

These vignettes represent a cross section of Hollywood writers, some working in feature films, others laboring in television, some trying to bridge the gap between the two areas. The issues these individuals face are similar to those experienced by other writers in Hollywood today, dilemmas that will be examined in the pages ahead. But before examining the present, it is necessary to briefly review the issues of the past.

Notes

[1]One psychiatrist who dealt specifically with the creative and personal problems of writers was interviewed. He indicated that these individuals were quick to seek psychotherapy and rarely resistant during the course of treatment. They committed to long-term therapy or returned to therapy over the years during personal crises.

Chapter Three

✦ ✦ ✦

Writers' Past

Early Hollywood was a rowdy, unpolished world composed of camera men, editors, technicians, and directors. Actors were told what parts to play as directors choreographed the action and hoped for the best. The only screenwriters required in the makeshift organization of silent filmmaking were gag writers and title makers who could sketch out a scene right before it was to be shot. Advance planning was nonexistent; plot and character were minor concerns.

The advent of the "talkies," motion pictures with sound, brought changes to Hollywood as the industry moved beyond the haphazard world of silent filmmaking and unplanned production. In the late 1920s, producers began to recognize the need for having scripts prepared before filming began. At the same time, the perfection of movie sound made dialogue an important feature in future films, affording screenwriters an enhanced role in the production process. By the early 1930s, studios were energetically recruiting writers to work in the industry. Numerous authors composed the cadre of screenwriters and story editors in Hollywood during this era, including such figures as Raymond Chandler, William Faulkner, F. Scott Fitzgerald, Dorothy Parker, Dashiell Hammett, Clifford Odets, and Lillian Hellman as well as expatriates Thomas Mann, Christopher Isherwood, and Bertolt Brecht. The combined promise of California and the security of a studio contract lured novelists, playwrights, and journalists west. For many, the promise was at least partially fulfilled. During the height of the Depression, Hollywood writers earned up to $100,000 a year. In addition, living and working in Hollywood provided a valuable source of material for later fiction. The genre of the Hollywood novel developed from the experiences of these writers (for example, O'Hara's 1938 *Hope of Heaven*).

However, there were grave problems for the individuals who came to the west coast with visions of good times and easy money. The

Hollywood contract system, while guaranteeing employment and inflated salaries for "name" screenwriters, functioned as a glorified assembly line. During work hours that ran from 9:00 to 6:00 p.m. on weekdays and 9:00 to 12:00 Saturdays, individuals tried to meet rigid deadlines and arbitrary demands. Their output was carefully controlled. At many studios, writers were required to hand in a prescribed number of pages each week or face dismissal. In addition, their physical environment was uncomfortable and hardly conducive to sustained productivity. Writers' offices were crowded and considered the least desirable on the studio lot. In these surroundings, writers encountered the group that would prove to be their nemesis in the industry: the producers. In fact, it has been their relationship with producers, more than directors, that has shaped writers' experience in Hollywood.

Although power ultimately rested with the studio moguls, producers acted as the foremen of the studio system. Depending on their status within the studio hierarchy, every screenwriter was assigned to a producer and a project. Writers exerted no choice in these assignments. It made no difference if the proposed script was a disaster or the producer a tyrant, little could be done. If a writer expressed the wish *not* to work with a particular producer or on a specific project, he was suspended without pay pending the dispute's resolution. Such practices acted as a strong control on writer rebellion; most writers accepted the arrangements studios made.

The arbitrary assignment of writing projects foreshadowed what occurred during the remainder of the production process. In the studio system, turning an idea into an actual motion picture involved a complicated ritual that appeared deliberately designed to drive writers crazy. Writers were first required to synopsize a property in five to ten pages for the producer to review. If the producer was pressed for time, the synopsis was reduced to one page or, in extreme cases, a paragraph.[1] Once the producer approved the synopsis, the writer was subjected to an agonizing round of story conferences involving the studio's supervising producer, the film's producer, potential directors, story editors, and anyone else whose input was deemed necessary. As the writer made his way through longer treatments to the shooting script, each step involved a grim repetition of the same process with more conferences, suggested revisions, and rewrites until some sort of "final" script reached completion. However, "final" was a misleading term. The screenwriting process rarely ended at this point. Instead, there were several potential denouements. A script might be shelved or "forgotten." Other writers might be called in to polish the already finished work. Scripts written by one writer were then rewritten by several additional writers. In an especially Kafkaesque turn of events, several writers would work on the identical script, all completely unaware of one another's existence. And in the end, the producer served as the ultimate arbiter, deciding which screenplay would be used and which writer would receive credit.

Obviously, screenwriters exerted little control over script content or screen credits. With many individuals working on the identical script, anywhere from one to ten writers could be involved in a fight for acknowledgment once a movie was produced. To further complicate matters, actors as well as directors often claimed writing credit. To appease the warring parties, producers often awarded screen credits in excess. Titles appeared in an endless list which detailed "screenplay by...," "from a story by...," "from an original idea by...," and "adapted by..." until the names blurred. The ultimate result of such maneuvering was a less than satisfying professional situation. For most writers, work in the script factory remained far removed from achieving artistic fulfillment.

The studio system emphasized quantity, not quality, with a solid commercial justification for such a philosophy. The entertainment industry was responsible for producing 500 films a year to satisfy audiences responding to motion pictures. As they concentrated on trying to meet this public demand, producers and studio executives scarcely considered nurturing their contract writers' creativity. The profits experienced by studios reinforced the assembly line mentality with the system thriving throughout the 1930s. Even mediocre films made money at the box office. This "Golden Age" of Hollywood provided studio chieftains with an illusion of indestructibility.

This illusion collapsed once the studio system came under attack. Many individuals chafed at how studios operated as "closed shops," exercising complete control over the professional and even personal lives of their employees. Agreements could be cancelled, pay cuts instituted and credits rewarded or revoked, all at the discretion of studio executives and producers. The contract system was criticized as mediocre and inefficient. When screenwriter Dalton Trumbo defiantly stated that "leeches...have sucked a young and vigorous industry into a state of almost total paresis" (qtd. in Schwartz 6), he was fingering the producers and calling for a change in the structure of Hollywood.

Trumbo, and others like him, proposed that the contract system be eliminated and in its place, a schedule of reasonable salaries and profit-sharing be established for writers, directors, and actors. Instead of being assigned to projects, individuals would be "free to work only in those pictures which, in their judgment will be successful" (Schwartz 7). If a writer rejected an assignment, he suffered the consequences without fear of studio reprisals. This idea, which many writers believed would raise movie quality and lower studio costs, angered the producers whose financial gain depended on expenses charged to a film's budget. It also threatened the unchallenged authority they had enjoyed in the studio system. The producers and writers squared off and the fight began.

The Hollywood writers' challenge to the studio system and producers involved a long struggle, complicated enough to warrant a study of its own.[2] Many individuals gambled with their futures, abandoning their contract arrangements to try and negotiate better terms. A number of writers expressed reluctance to take such a drastic step, insisting that the studios had been good to them. However, once it became evident that in a freelance arrangement the potential rewards far outweighed the risks, most screenwriters decided it was time to "leave home." These individuals did not surrender the relative security of the studio system without any sort of alternative structure. To bolster their confidence and represent their interests in all arbitration, writers did exactly what the producers anticipated—and dreaded. They formed an organization.

The Screenwriters Guild was founded in 1933.[3] For nearly nine years producers fought the Guild, the proposed freelance arrangements and the rebelling writers, using every tactic at their disposal. But their actions only delayed the ultimate outcome. In 1941 Hollywood producers recognized the Guild. Writers won a minimum fee schedule and the right to arbitrate credits. Later, in the era of television, they would also win the right to arbitrate residuals. But producers won ownership of story rights, a concession that foreshadowed future losses writers would suffer. Nevertheless, the recognition of the Guild was a momentous achievement for Hollywood writers. Powerless as individuals, they had marshaled bargaining power as a group.

After the establishment of the Writers Guild, the studio system suffered its final setback when the 1950 Supreme Court ruled that studio ownership of movie theater chains constituted restraint of trade. Further problems arose when the introduction of television into American households began to threaten the monopoly moviemakers had held over audience attention. These events combined to create an atmosphere filled with possibility.

Hollywood power politics became fluid, control was negotiable. Writers obtained contracts for specific projects rather than time periods. They could exert at least some control in selecting what they wrote. Unfortunately, the change in the Hollywood structure was incomplete. While superficially negotiations had replaced the assembly line, writers discovered they still had to contend with the studio hierarchy who controlled financing. Studio producers unhappy with the new arrangement continued to interfere and impose their authority, often offering inappropriate suggestions or restructuring scripts with last-minute changes. Additionally, the studios and producers began to search for a new way to bring writers under control.

Surprisingly, the answer to their dilemma was evolving in Washington, D.C. The 1950s brought Senator Joseph McCarthy's search for Communists to Hollywood. Many prominent screenwriters were identified as Communists, often by producers who appeared anxious to prove their own innocence. The impact of this now infamous "witch hunt" was profound. From 1947 to 1960 a blacklist existed with the Hollywood Ten,[4] as well as other less-known writers, prevented from working in the industry. A more virulent form of social control could not have been invented by the producers themselves. In order to survive financially, many writers left the industry altogether. Others chose a more convoluted method of making a living: they hired a go-between or "front." The front received an assignment and later delivered a completed screenplay to the studio, for a price. The actual writers knocked out screenplays for bargain fees, using pseudonyms for screen credits. Industry insiders, completely aware of what was happening, allowed the deception. In one of Hollywood's most open secrets, black-listed screenwriter Dalton Trumbo won the 1956 Academy Award for best original story as "Robert Rich." To exacerbate the insult, prior to being blacklisted Trumbo had been one of the highest paid screenwriters in the industry. He now worked for reduced fees. In this atmosphere of hypocrisy and paranoia, blacklisting continued, unchallenged. Finally in 1960 when—ironically enough—Dalton Trumbo received formal screen credits for the films *Spartacus* and *Exodus*, blacklisting officially ended.

The question remains of why blacklisting occurred in the first place. In addition, the blacklist's endurance beyond the McCarthy era has given rise to alternative theories concerning its existence. Many in Hollywood have argued that producers simply used McCarthy and the HUAC as a vehicle for re-establishing their control in the industry. Producers did not care about Communists, they simply wanted to intimidate the rebelling writers, curbing the power of the Guild. As early as the 1930s, producers linked screenwriters' efforts at establishing a collective bargaining organization with Communist leanings. This effort at discrediting writers laid the groundwork for the blacklist of the 1950s. It tests the claims of coincidence that several of the most outspoken and influential screenwriters, many of them instrumental in the organization of the Writers Guild, were broken once they were blacklisted. How much studio executives and producers can be held culpable for what took place remains unclear.

Although blacklisting eventually ended, the diminished status of Hollywood writers endured. Real power still managed to elude their grasp. Whatever writers achieved in the industry remained secondary to the powers others enjoyed. In addition, the writers' position was always susceptible to attack. The next effort at undermining Hollywood writers was not launched by an opportunistic politician like McCarthy but by an artistic theory originating in Europe. The "auteur" theory, introduced by Godard, Truffaut, Rohmer, Chabrol, and others, held that the *real* author or "auteur" of a film was not the writer but the director. These critics, writing for the French publication *Cahiers du Cinema* insisted that the director created films out of his experience and served as the guiding force in cinematic art. This idea gave birth to an entire era of personalized French filmmaking labeled the "New Wave," which included the work of Jean-Luc Godard, Louis Malle, Eric Rohmer, among others, including Truffaut himself. According to those in the "auteur" school, American moviemaking had yet to realize its artistic potential. Until directors assumed control and were allowed to truly "author" films, American cinema could never be taken seriously as "art."

The theory provoked heated debate. Some film reviewers argued that the auteur theory was culturally more appropriate to Europe, where directors often worked independent of studios with smaller budgets and an organizational structure in which they actually wrote the screenplays for their films. American filmmaking required an altogether different approach: a collaborative effort dependent on studio support. Still many critics latched on to the auteur theory, perhaps seeking the opportunity to act as kingmakers. Critics played favorites with different directors and indiscriminately praised the films made by their pet "auteurs." The cult of the director grew to an extreme in which, according to Richard Corliss, directors were awarded not only authorship but ownership of films. In addition to the critics, many individuals who worked in Hollywood defended or attacked the auteur theory, their arguments usually determined by self-interest. Certainly, it was not surprising that Hollywood directors enthusiastically embraced auteurism. But writers resented this further denial of what they considered *their* role as the rightful authors or auteurs of films. They voiced disapproval of the theory, claiming its adherents in the industry betrayed how little even Hollywood insiders understood the filmmaking process.

Like any new idea that has provoked intense reaction, the auteur theory soon wore thin, and the controversy surrounding it receded. At the end of the 1960s, auteur theory was passé. Still, the screenwriters' fundamental dilemma of being necessary but undervalued remained unresolved. Many writers rebelled against their "second class" standing. They demanded recognition and more creative control. Following the pattern they set in their first struggles with producers, writers turned once again to the Guild for support. During the 1960s, the Writers Guild first emerged as the main force behind the writers' fight to achieve enhanced respect within the entertainment industry.

To understand the Guild's role in Hollywood writers' past and present, it is necessary to know Guild organization. The membership of the Guild is broken into two branches: the Writers Guild East and the Writers Guild West. In order to join, the Guild requires that an individual sell a property to an industry representative, although the work does not have to be produced. The Guild also registers original materials, arbitrates writer-agent disputes, maintains a credit union, offers group health and life insurance benefits and a variety of other services, including an office for the "support of freedom of expression." The Writers Guild is affiliated with other American film groups (for example, the American Film Institute, the Motion Picture and Television Relief Fund) as well as international groups (for example, the Australian Writers Guild and the Writers Guild of Great Britain).

The Writers Guild, however, exists first and foremost as a union, intent on insuring its members' rights to adequate financial compensation for a completed work, even if that work is never produced. If a work enters production, the Writers Guild confirms that proper credits are awarded. The Guild establishes minimum terms for contract negotiations, credits, and fees for services rendered. The Guild also possesses the power to organize strikes when its governing board decides that financial compensations and related rights merit revision or strengthening.

Drawing on its power to call strikes and organize member actions, over the past three decades the WGA gradually assumed the role of a catalyst for political activism and change. While the specific issues evolved over time, the status of Hollywood screenwriters remained the underlying cause. In 1960 a strike initiated by the Guild lasted five months, winning writers residuals from *network* television.

This victory put producers on notice that the twin problems of money and creative control would figure prominently in all future negotiations. Rebounding from their impotence in the face of HUAC investigations, from 1960 on, the Guild was quick to call for walkouts, demonstrations, and long-term strikes. However, these sporadic political actions produced little substantial change. The producers rarely yielded to writers' demands and industry power appeared impermeable. Still the Guild directors and membership remained optimistic. Then in 1981 things began to unravel.

It started simply enough. The Guild organized a strike which lasted 13 weeks, aimed at guaranteeing writers residuals from *pay* television. At its resolution, the Guild declared the action a success, winning writers future revenues from the newly established pay-TV market. But pay television failed to gain mass acceptance; writers never enjoyed the promised profits. Instead they ended up paying a very high price for their demands. Not only did the strike prove financially devastating for most Guild members, deeper, more serious consequences were soon to be felt. As a result of this strike, the Guild itself began to fragment.

In the 1981 walkout, the WGA leadership had insisted on and received extensive member participation. When the strike ultimately failed to produce any lasting changes, many individuals became enraged. Dissident voices spoke out and opposition groups organized. For the first time, writers' anger was directed at a target other than producers. They blamed their own Guild. Many writers moved to curb the Guild's tendency to call strikes indiscriminately while failing to consider the needs of its membership. But screenwriter dissatisfaction did not stop with the issue of picket lines. The Guild was also blamed for the chronic problem of underemployment, a charge that was unfounded. Statistically speaking, each year more writers join the Guild, while job opportunities remain at 1958 levels. With such intense competition for so few positions, most Guild members cannot earn a living as writers. Indeed, 80 percent of the Guild membership earn less than $15,000 a year. Blaming the Guild for the situation was unfair, at best. At worst, it shifted the focus away from the producers who were capable of actually altering the problem of underemployment by opening opportunities to more writers on various projects. The producers happily shared the blame, amused at the turn of events. Instead of focusing on the producers as the problem, writers fought among themselves. In directing their anger and frustration towards the Guild, writers did little more than put both past and present Guild directors on the defensive. When former Guild president Christopher Knopf protested that writers had a "right to be terrified and very angry. But it is not the Guild's fault," his words made little impact. Writers grew progressively more apathetic about voting, attending meetings, and participating in Guild activities. An increasing number of members resisted striking.

The conflicts troubling the Guild came out in the open when the 1984-85 arbitration and strike ended in disaster. In April 1984 the WGA initiated 51 labor arbitrations against 17 film companies, seeking back payment for royalties owed to writers for videocassette rentals. But before labor arbitration was underway, the Guild leadership also called a strike against producers, a move both ill-conceived and miscalculated. Producers stalled their response to arbitration into 1985 when their videocassette royalty contract with the WGA expired. The contract ran out and the producers then held an extra chip to deal, giving them an advantage over writers at the bargaining table. The strike dragged on and the speedy victory Guild leadership had predicted vanished with the passage of time.

The reaction of the Writers Guild membership to all of this was direct and negative. The Writers Guild East threatened to cross picket lines. Lionel Chetwynd, a distinguished writer who had worked in Hollywood for years, organized the "Union Blues," a group spearheading the opposition to the Guild Board of Directors. Chetwynd spoke for many when he claimed that every strike had a "hidden agenda," explaining, "I really understand what a writers' strike does...it basically kills all the people coming out. The established people do very well out of it... (Grant 1). At this point, with its membership questioning the Guild's motives in general as well as the current action in particular, the strike was doomed. When balloting was called, writers voted overwhelmingly to accept the producers' terms, including a less favorable interpretation of the videocassette royalty guidelines. The financial battle was lost. But worse still, the Guild was in disarray.

The 1985 Guild elections marked a turning point. Fighting reached an intense level, with both leadership and membership divided on key issues. Writers expressed a constant sense of dissatisfaction, portraying the Guild as anachronistic, elitist and ineffective. David Rintels, another former Guild president delivered a chilling obituary when he observed, "the Guild isn't simply dying...it's being devoured from within" (Horn 14).

Despite these dire reports, the Guild endured its leadership crisis. From 1985 on, conflict diminished and new members were elected to the board of directors. Reassuring their membership its needs came first, the WGA returned to confronting its old adversary: the producers. In the spring of 1988, the Guild once again engaged in a protracted strike against producers—an action lasting five months. At issue were residuals and creative control. Unfortunately, the strike was long, costly and produced little substantive change. But the Guild membership united in support of the leaders who called the strike. Opposition to the strike surfaced only in the waning days of the action, when it appeared writers were getting nowhere with their demands. When producers threatened to use scabs, foreign writers—anyone—to get the industry moving again, the strike moved more rapidly to resolution. In retrospect, the dynamics of the 1988 strike appeared all too familiar. The writers were cast once again as the children, petulantly throwing a temper tantrum. The producers, with patience and adult equanimity, indulged them for awhile. However, when the "business" of Hollywood had been inconvenienced a little too long, the producers threatened punishment and the Guild conceded. The writers gained little except a reputation for making trouble. The producers remained in control.

At times, little appears to have changed since the "golden age" of Hollywood. At that time, the industry was smaller and the competition less intense. But the producers prevailed in control, with writers simply the hired help—occasionally squabbling and struggling for power. Today, despite Hollywood's corporate structure and high financial stakes, the basic problems continue. The producers hold money and power, the writers want more. Battles have been fought over specific issues: the Guild, the blacklist, auteurism, residuals, credits, and creative authority. But all of these fights have really been about one thing: writers achieving the professional standing they believe they have earned.

Notes

[1]Forty years later John Gregory Dunne described reducing script synopses to one sentence for producer Joseph Levine. The film, *The Panic in Needle Park*, was financed based on the one-line description "Romeo and Juliet on junk" (Dunne 1980: 188).

[2]In fact, the late Nancy Lynn Schwartz's *The Hollywood Writers' Wars* (1982) is an excellent account of what occurred during this era.

[3]In 1954 the Screenwriters Guild joined the Radio Writers Guild to form the Writers Guild of America (WGA). From this point on the organization will be referred to as the Writers Guild or WGA.

[4]The Hollywood Ten were: Alvah Bessie, Herbert Biberman, Lester Cole, Edward Dymtryk, Ring Lardner, Jr., John Howard Lawson, Albert Maltz, Samuel Ornitz, Robert Adrian Scott, and Dalton Trumbo.

Chapter Four

✦ ✦ ✦

To Write in Hollywood
You Have to Be Short and Jewish

Perhaps because Hollywood undervalues writers, several individuals I interviewed went to great lengths to demonstrate their importance, as illustrated by one typical encounter with a successful film writer. During an initial telephone contact, this writer detailed his pressing schedule then specified the day, time, and locale of our meeting, warning that if he did not like me, he would end the interview after five minutes. His admonition served as the prelude to a nightmare of control. He arrived 30 minutes late and without explaining, he asked to switch seats. Once we exchanged places I understood why; his new seat afforded him a view of the room, which was filled with actors, producers and other writers eating at adjacent tables. The five-minute test passed without incident, but during the interview we were repeatedly interrupted by people stopping at our table on their way out. The writer calmly conducted business while the interview proceeded, lining up pitch meetings, tennis dates, and dinner arrangements with different individuals who spoke with him. Several other writers, while not this controlling, also set the tone and limits of their interviews. Complaining about their busy schedules, they demanded particular days, times, meeting places, and time limits. In some cases, secretaries reconfirmed interviews. But once interviews were underway, these same writers talked for hours and often offered to meet me again; time limits were suspended.

What type of person exemplifies the majority of writers at work in Hollywood today? To begin with, the personal histories of the many people I met with were almost hauntingly uniform. With chagrin, many writers referred to the normality of their background. One writer sighed and said, "I'd love to tell you it was like *Long Day's Journey Into Night*

39

growing up but the truth is, my childhood was so boring you wouldn't believe it—it was more like something out of *Father Knows Best* with a Jewish twist."

These writers brought reality to the stereotype: most of them were, in fact, Jewish. The majority of Anglo writers interviewed identified themselves as Jews, immediately adding they felt more culturally than religiously Jewish. Such an identification undoubtedly received reinforcement in Hollywood, where many creative and management personnel are Jewish and the unofficial language is Yiddish (McClintick; Litwak). They described modest upbringings with, as one writer recalled, "one foot in the shtetl and one foot in the suburbs." Several writers emphasized the immigrant or traditional Jewish roots they sprang from, contrasting the simplicity of their upbringing with the complexity of modern life. But except for these broad sketches, family life received little attention. Majority writers' personal revelations consisted of humorous anecdotes relating parental reaction to having offspring working in Hollywood. Writers rarely discussed their spouses and often revealed they were married or divorced only indirectly in the course of the interview.

Their innocuous descriptions of family life centered on rather neutral considerations: their concern for their own children and children in general, their dismay at the current atmosphere of urban violence and economic uncertainty, and the question of international instability in the Middle East and Eastern Europe. However, these writers openly discussed their internal conflicts. Every majority writer interviewed mentioned experience in therapy. While many failed to specify the extent of their involvement, interviews were peppered with references to "my therapist" or "my analyst." Majority writers experienced anxiety in their lives and claimed they wanted to use whatever means available to work through it. Their primary concern was how much their personal conflict affected their writing.

Despite their involvement with their craft, individuals made little mention of any contact with a "community of writers," and talked about the Writers Guild primarily in disparaging terms. These writers depicted themselves as apathetic about Guild politics and uninvolved in activism. "I make it a policy never to vote in any Guild elections," one writer virtually bragged. "Whether it's for the Board of Directors or someone's latest idea of why we should strike. They're just so beside the point."

Several writers reinforced this idea, referring to the Guild as "a joke" or "impotent." None of the majority writers appeared to take the Guild too seriously, many offering a view of Guild activities as a "waste of time" and "running opposite a writer's best interests: their work."

In terms of preparing for Hollywood, education and youth proceeded hand in hand: the younger the writer, the more formal education completed. Most older writers reported some college experience, although not all had finished degrees. Every writer under 35 had completed college, some continuing to acquire graduate degrees. These men received at least some training through theater arts programs; their initial experiences with screenwriting had occurred under the tutelage of college instructors who were often screenwriters themselves. The university education and a college degree distinguished "younger" from "older" writers. It was, however, no guarantee of success.

Whatever their particular background, for most writers their first order of business had been "breaking in" to Hollywood. Several men interviewed did not join the screenwriting ranks immediately and were forced to work at other jobs to support themselves in the interim. They attempted to obtain industry-related work, pursuing these positions energetically out of the belief that any such post could conceivably provide access to the world of film or television. Still, several writers recalled working as waiters or tutors and talked about their strong desire to "get in" or to "return" to the industry as soon as possible, writing in their spare time. Everyone emphasized the importance of networking and industry contacts. "You have to be tough," one writer explained.

And you can't be intimidated by the Hollywood bullshit. A friend of mine was story editing and I ran into him at a party. I told him some ideas and he said, "That's pretty good, call me, I'll get you an appointment." So I called him. He won't take the phone call. So I reached him at home and I said, "I called you," and he said, "Well, I'll tell the producer you're going to call." And I said, "Do me a favor, make the appointment for me, get me on the lot, introduce me to the producer." So finally he did that...I had a meeting with the producer. The producer's an alcoholic—I found out...but he listens to my material and he says, "I love it, call me next week." I called him and he never returned the call. And I called him just to get him upset, every single day for about 90 days. I left my name, he never called me back...Now that's an extreme example, but it's very stereotypical today. You're either in or you're out and they won't take a chance on you.

It was here that screenwriters emphasized luck. Making it in the industry was never simply a matter of talent. In fact, it was virtually a proviso that in order to succeed in Hollywood, one had to possess talent, contacts, *and* luck in the right combination. Several experienced writers viewed luck as the crucial factor. "I could have easily ended up doing something else," one told me, "I just got lucky." This reliance on luck grew more pronounced among older writers. One veteran screenwriter explained:

At the very beginning I really had to go to work. I had three children and no job, so anything I could get, I just really worked my ass off and for three years when I couldn't get employment, I really tried to learn the business. I stole every script I could get. I read it. I analyzed it. I wrote outlines. I couldn't sell them— I talked to people and finally *I got lucky*. Someone gave me a chance. When I finally got connected—I thought Hollywood was wonderful. And once I got started, I worked a lot and I won awards later on and I got well established. I was lucky. It was difficult. And it's worse today than it was then.

Another writer commented, "I was a 'hack' for years. I used to write what they would call 'B' movies. I don't know why they called me to write on that particular project—they probably drew my name out of a hat. I guess God was smiling on me or something—there's really no other explanation. I was goddamned lucky."

These responses, typical of writers over 35, differed markedly from the experiences of younger writers. These men, most frequently those who had graduated from theater arts or film programs, described more exact career plans. They explained how they had established themselves in Hollywood and also offered their future professional agendas. According to one writer:

Through a friend, the first thing I knew I had to do was get an agent. That was impossible but I finally found someone willing to take me at William Morris. He wasn't Michael Ovitz though, and what I really had to do was call everyone I went through school with, to try to find out who was working where, and just bother the shit out of everyone, get them to read my scripts, offer to write things for nothing and always, always, try to meet someone else. It worked—and I guess my writing was fairly good. Then I got a partner who had already sold some stuff and we wrote a script together and his agent and my agent got together and next thing I knew we had a deal. Of course, now that I've sold a pilot, the next thing I've got to do is make a deal for a series. I don't want to stay in television forever and the best thing is, I want to meet someone in TV who's looking to move to features—I'll go along with them.

The emphasis on individual control and planned action prevailed among majority writers under 35. Older writers underplayed their achievements partly because, according to one, "the industry has changed and the competition has increased. It's not like the old days." Several writers recalled the Hollywood of the past with affection. There were relaxed meetings with producers and a Guild half its current size. Most importantly, there was an oversupply of work, with some writers handling more than one assignment at a given time. In an account freighted with nostalgia, one writer reminisced that "it was a club, it was great." Hollywood sounded less like a corporate enterprise and more like a cottage industry.

Today there is little sign of such cooperation in the industry, if it ever existed in the first place. Competition has intensified as screenwriters' ranks have expanded. The same writer who waxed nostalgic about the "club" atmosphere of Hollywood continued:

Today—I am trying to help a young writer get started who's a brilliant writer, a little awkward as a person but he's a brilliant writer, and I've helped him develop into a terrific writer...but he can't get a job, his wife just got pregnant, he's been trying three years to get his career going, people love his material but they never call him back...and I don't know why. That's the way the business is...it all depends on luck.

Three veteran screenwriters agreed that professional opportunities are severely limited compared with times past. Still, majority writers insist, "breaking in" is not the biggest problem screenwriters face today. Staying in is. It is difficult for writers to maintain their positions "inside" an industry that is fickle, at best. "You're either in or you're out," more than one writer told me. One individual elaborated:

You can go right to the top very quickly. Let's say you're a young writer and they take a chance with you on a show like "Seinfeld" and you do well. They give you another assignment and you do well. They make you a story editor right away, give you an executive job, load you down with work because, quote "You can do our show, nobody else can do it, you're one of the few people who can do our show." The whole secret to doing the show is being on the inside and you know what's going on. You know what you can do, what you can't do, you're in the meetings, you get very familiar with it. That's how easy it is— once you're there to stay. But staying is the tricky part.

Despite such difficulties, however, these writers did not perceive the system as blocked or inaccessible. Quite the contrary—majority writers asserted that reality in Hollywood was always subject to change. The producer who rejected their pitches could just as easily be in professional disfavor—and out of a job—the next time they arrived to peddle a script. The fluid and fickle atmosphere of Hollywood worked to their advantage. Even for those who based their success on luck, there was a bright side—bad luck could certainly change.

Additionally, the majority writers did not cast the entertainment industry as an adversary. When plans were thwarted or opportunities denied, these individuals did not pause to distribute blame. They concentrated on action rather than rationalization. Such pragmatism extended to their future planning. Based on their Hollywood experiences, several majority writers outlined strategies for making contacts and advancing professionally. "It's always important, you've got to be able to meet the right people at the network and—yes—impress them," one writer admitted:

It's no use spending time and energy on someone who can't get something through for you, who won't buy a project or give you money for development. You've got to meet the people who can green light a project for you—or at least know someone who can green light a project. Of course, it's a tricky thing because people are always being hired and fired, no one stays in one place too long. But if you make a connection, sooner or later that guy's going to turn up somewhere where he can do you some good, or at least you don't want him doing you any harm.

Another writer outlined his plans for obtaining and consolidating power:

I guess you probably would already guess what I want to do. I don't want to write forever. I want to produce and direct. But I can't just do it, not because I say so. Wishing doesn't make it all come true. This sounds really premeditated but it's all got to be carefully planned. I've got to have my writing read and produced by the right people. It's true, it's a matter of "right time, right place," but I want to make sure that my chances of being in that right place at the right time are the greatest. And you can only do that when you meet and end up working with the right people. I need the right people interested in my project, name people—because you get power in Hollywood by being associated with them. It's like the people with Spielberg. Now you may not know their names, but guys in Hollywood do. And people figure if you work with Spielberg or Oliver Stone or Adrian Lyne, you know something, you've got something, and maybe it'll rub off on them. So they want you and they're willing to give you things, maybe even *some* power. It all works out.

Writers' success frequently depended on inside information. Once they gained access, writers invariably focused their energies on being well-informed industry gossips. Unfortunately, what they learned frequently reinforced their already negative views. Many writers disparaged Hollywood and anyone who chose to work there. At times, they deprecated themselves along with everyone else. This deprecation, at its most extreme, invariably alluded to the greed and desire for financial gain they felt they shared. One writer remarked, "In Hollywood, we're all basically whores."

However, beyond such negativity, these writers displayed an uncanny sense of Hollywood and how it operated, their observations assuming an almost clinical tone. Many offered an objective—and exhaustive—overview of the industry. Additionally, writers could discuss budget, production costs, "above the line" and "below the line" accounting, and the conundrum of media finance with the acumen of corporate executives.

When they talked about Hollywood, writers expressed respect for power. They vented little hostility towards those who possessed ultimate power, the studio and network executives. Instead majority writers' anger was reserved for the middle line, moderately powerful individuals who exerted direct control over their work: directors, censors, actors, and line producers. Indeed, when explaining why he found particularly powerful executives the easiest to deal with, one writer succinctly stated, "The higher up you go, the less bullshit you'll get."

In terms of their own membership in the Hollywood elite, writers feigned indifference but revealed a subtle pleasure at being "on the inside." They enjoyed discussing famous actors and "players," offering gossip and dropping names throughout interviews. The most successful majority writer interviewed was also the most indiscriminate name dropper in the sample. He was not alone. Every majority writer identified celebrities and powerful executives as personal friends. They divulged intimate anecdotes, carefully prefacing their remarks with requests that such revelations be "off the record." In addition, industry alliances constituted a source of pride. One veteran screenwriter discussed his relationship with an infamous studio executive stating, "He's a great guy, he bought me my 500 SL [Mercedes]. We are really close friends and I love him...but everything they tell you about him is true and I know worse. He'd give you the shirt off his back—but then he'd take the shirt off your back without telling you if he needed it. And if you froze to death, he'd laugh."

Understanding and ultimately accepting the structure of the business freed majority writers to concentrate on individual and internal concerns. The "suits"—executives and producers—were perceived as a necessary evil to be dealt with periodically. Of course, agents existed to ease such interactions. Although they worried about gaining access to Hollywood, and surviving once there, Anglo writers' main concern remained the fate of their work.

Their personal investment in screenwriting was not something these writers admitted easily. They invariably began with denials of any emotional involvement, emphasizing that writing was business, nothing "personal." However, as interviews proceeded it became clear that even screenwriting, at least for some of these men, was an extremely personal endeavor. Their emotional lives and previous experiences, as well as their dreams and expectations, influenced their work, serving as a creative resource. Many writers described how they used the writing process to "work through" conflicts and dilemmas. One veteran television writer, who initially claimed his only interest in screenwriting stemmed from the lucrative income Hollywood provided, later launched into a discussion of his actual work. He poetically described characters he created for motion pictures and television, insisting that the characters came from "real life" and resembled people he knew, taken to ideal types. He outlined script ideas that sprang from problems he had encountered in marriage, divorce and raising adolescent offspring with drug problems and eating disorders. The writer repeatedly contradicted his initial claim that writing was simply business and ended up soliloquizing about violence, the Rodney King trials, and Hollywood's influence on what he termed "the quality of life." His remarks illustrated an inconsistency frequent among screenwriters: despite disclaimers, these writers were strongly invested in their scripts. "My scripts are my fantasies coming to life," one writer confessed. "That's what every screenwriter does, whether he knows it or not. He gets to bring his dreams to the public and if he's good at what he does, the public watches and shares and identifies with his fantasy."

Several majority writers described the relationship between personal identity and their writing. "I've never wanted to grow up," one writer openly admitted, "I guess my writing keeps me a little boy in my fantasy world where I can have everything as I want it. There is no loss and there is no pain—or if I'm writing a melodrama and there *is* loss and pain, I get to control it, I get to know how it turns out. Life's not like that—but my script can be."

"I've been married four times and lived with women in between. I'm still looking for the perfect woman," another writer laughed. "When I got a chance to write my last screenplay, I finally got to make the perfect woman. It was great. Now I'll never have to get married again. I've got her."

Several writers emphasized the importance of writing about something real, that effective screenplays read as if events had been personally "experienced," not simply "written." No less than Neil Simon characterized screenwriting as "something that comes from that place inside us that is common truth" (Brady 344). Similarly, Paddy Chayefsky once depicted the writer's aim as "trying to create a moment of life that people will believe" (Brady 60). Most majority writers enthusiastically agreed with these observations. One writer, extremely successful in the industry, interrupted questioning to exclaim:

I put a lot of myself into my writing. A lot, a lot. *That's all I have.* See, it's the pleasure I get when I work, that's the fun. Once the outline is agreed upon and you go to work on the characters and they begin to lead their own lives and they're talking to you and you're talking to them and you're writing them and you're writing a mother who's got a very advanced view of life, you're talking to her daughter, who's very old-fashioned, and you suddenly switched—the role reversal thing—and it works, and you say to yourself, "Gee, this is really the way to do this. This scene has a little sparkle, a little vitality," and you don't have to tell the audience, "this is a modern woman and an old-fashioned daughter," they sense it, they don't know why they like this scene but they do.

Other writers reinforced the importance of personal experience. "What else have you got?" one writer asked. "And what else have you got in common to share with that audience but your humanity, your humanness. Maybe I write about a particular problem I had with my kids and some poor slob out there has a similar problem and he can identify. I can embroider on it and elaborate but what else is there really to write about except that same old shit we all face day in and day out in living our lives." Another writer stated:

Sure I draw upon things that happen to me. Sometimes I've used them over and over. Disguised them. But there are a few events in my life I've used many times, sometimes with a male character, sometimes with a female character, sometimes with an older person, younger person. Significant events that have moved me...I think that's the only time you're successful, when you use that personal experience.

Majority writers all were quick to add that they camouflaged personal experience when writing. One writer based a feature film screenplay on his own tumultuous divorce—in a scarcely recognizable form. "In the script there was no divorce," he explained. "Instead the wife dies. And the man has got to adjust. And he's got children living with him. In point of fact, my children stayed with my wife. But my screenplay was more a 'Mr. Mom' sort of thing—without any ex-wife re-entering the picture. I think in a funny way writing that script helped convince me, helped me convince myself, that my kids were better off with my ex-wife." Most writers practiced disguise ingeniously, including one who stated:

I use my own life experiences as the basis for most scripts. But I don't want things turning into a roman à clef—no matter how limited the population I'm using is. If one person knows it's their personal life I'm using, things could get messy. So there are all kinds of tricks to disguise this—turn men into women and vice versa, children into adults, losses into gains. Underneath, I know the real meaning and by the time it's produced, it's so hacked up anyway, no one knows the difference.

Writers modified and combined segments of different experiences in creating characters and plots. Whatever the method of subterfuge, majority writers drew heavily upon personal experience as a source of ideas and inspiration.

Most writers admitted they encountered problems coming up with new ideas for screenplays and teleplays. One writer offered a detailed account of an idea's development:

Another writer told me that at one time many years ago he had written a short story which he had never published about these people who are experimented upon by the Army without their knowledge and how one guy jumped out a window hallucinating on LSD...and I thought to myself, "well, that's kind of old hat, we all know about that, but supposing that that happens to somebody and the spouse of that person is in a sense responsible for that without knowing it." And that's what I asked him. So we started with a guy who was at one time in a drug company, he was doing research on this thing and it had been taken away from him and they had kicked him upstairs or given him what was a better project, knowing that he was on the track of something that could be repressive in the area that they wanted to work in. And he sensed it but he was young and so now it comes back to haunt him and he says to himself, "Jesus, if I had only pursued that or done something about it, she'd still be alive today, it's my fault." So in a sense, that's what we're doing with it. So that idea came from outside.

Ideas could be culled from a variety of sources, some of them mundane. One writer offered that

...you go through your files, you look at *TV Guide* and *Variety* and *The Hollywood Reporter* and see what's being done. You get a feeling from talking to other people what might sell, you may call a network and say, "Can I just come in and get a feeling of what you want?" Or you ask the same question of some studio executive. And they say, "Well we are moving away from the area of male orientation to the female orientation" or "What we want is young, young people, gangs and cocaine, that type of thing." And then you go home and say to yourself, "Geez, what can I do?" And then there's always the routine stuff, the disease stories or it's an AIDS story or homicide or whatever. You try to figure out what you can write about that's interesting or different that is still going to be appealing.

These writers did not depend exclusively on their own resources for ideas. Many worked adapting books or other sources for television and feature films, a process that often grew complicated. One writer outlined his experience working on an adaptation:

They had a screenplay written by—I think it was the book's authors and it didn't turn out well—and he [the producer] was looking around for somebody and at that time he didn't have a lot of money to spend and he called my agent. My agent suggested he talk to me. So we talked and we got along well and he asked me to read the script...I said, "I don't want to read the script, I just want to read the book and let me tell you how I react to it." That's what I did. I read the book. I could see the script was a mess and I started all over. No use adapting what they had already botched. I started from scratch. Read the book again and wrote what turned out to be a pretty good film—for that genre.

For these writers, adapting a script from another medium, whether an article, book, news item, or short story, represented a different task than generating and developing an original idea. Adaptations were greeted with a certain degree of antipathy, although majority writers accepted the reality that at least *some* of their work would have to be of an "assignment nature." But even an undesirable project became interesting if the screenwriter was able to become invested in his work. Writers explained that when they felt personally involved in a screenplay, whether it was an original work or an adaptation, they were able to make use of personal experience extensively.

It was not enough to draw on personal experience, however. Writers insisted that such material had to be used appropriately, generating ideas, plots and characters that worked. Most majority writers insisted they knew when an idea was "right," describing their intuitions that story lines "flew," that dialogue felt "real." However, they were unable to elaborate on their intuitions. Writers relied on perceptions, unconscious or "gut" reactions more than rigid techniques. "I know it sounds stupid, but I don't know how to put it into words. If something is right, it just hits you—you know it!" one writer claimed. "You don't need to go any farther. I was working on a script once, revising, revising, revising, polishing. There was the point that I knew, it was finished. Or at least for me it was finished—there was nothing else to be done."

Writers occasionally referred to "techniques" and mentioned screenwriting manuals, with Syd Field touted as the author of the "bible" for beginning screenwriters. But in general, these men underemphasized writing methods, remained vague about specific practices and only spoke at length about the overall experience of writing. Typical was one writer's discourse:

There is, of course, the terror of the empty page but there is also that excitement when you're really going that you live for. Some people might tell you writing is painful process—even screenwriting. Once you're writing it's not painful at all. What's painful is when you're blocked and you can't think of anything— Jesus, I think the Guild actually has a support group for people with writers' block and other problems. The real problem is NOT writing. If you're working and writing and it's all coming out on paper and the characters are real and the plot is fitting together—even if you're writing a sitcom and just getting the lines to come out right—that's the greatest feeling in the world. It's like sex.

While the process of screenwriting posed difficulties at times, writers' enthusiasm for their work was greatest when they discussed the process of creating believable characters. Many claimed that the real work of writing for Hollywood did not occur with the invention of a plot but instead with characterization. "I think we try to make real characters as a way of getting back at producers and directors for taking over the control of our script," one writer explained.

The one thing that can live on in spite of any producer or director is a good character—or a good conception of a character. It's exactly the kind of thing they won't fool around with—it's the detail they'll leave alone. They don't care about some little nuance that I know is there—like the name of a character—so they won't change it. Meanwhile they'll do all kinds of things to the plot, people who are written to die of cancer wind up getting shot, people who are supposed to get shot wind up shooting someone else or protesting gun control, or any other thing that changes the plot content entirely. But meanwhile, they don't change the character's name or what he or she believes or what they say and I know it's there and it's mine.

Through characters, the writer exerted control over the script in absentia, preserving part of the story's original tone. While plot is susceptible to outside change and revision, memorable characters—or at the very least, their traits—may endure through a tangle of script revisions. With plot awarded to producers and directors, character development remains the last possession of writers. According to one:

I know that most writers try to get something of quality into the work that they do and sometimes it works and sometimes it doesn't. But the area in which you're most effective is not really in the theme or in the story but in the characters. In that area you can *do* something if you're so inclined. And you can make the individual character in a television show or a movie valid. And if that validity exists, people relate to that validity and presumably have some kind of reaction. It has some kind of effect.

Majority writers related to their audiences through the characters they created. "All writing is autobiographical," one writer declared. "And every single character a writer creates *is* that writer. It's sort of like dreams in a Freudian analysis. Y'know, every character in the dream is some element of the dreamer. Well, every character in a screenplay is some element of the writer." Another writer explained how characters distinguished particular scripts and enabled television and motion pictures to occasionally rise above mediocrity:

I think that's the only time you're successful. Because plot really doesn't make any difference. It's the people in the show who make the difference. On a good show you really don't need a lot of plot. I remember a film I did. And I remember a scene in which the marshal, after a hard day, comes back and is exhausted and he sits down in his chair outside the office, leans back against the wall and the old doc comes by, gets a chair and leans back against the wall next to him and they sit there without talking for a few minutes and the doctor says... "How did it go today, you look tired," and he says, "I had a terrible day," he said, "the weather was awful, my horse got lame, I just felt so tired." The doctor said, "I had the same feeling, the same problem, there's so and so across the street..." It had nothing to do with plot at all. And the scene is so vivid in my memory. These are two human being discussing the difficulties of life in the west. And the story stopped and they had this little interchange between these people whose lives were suddenly very real. But it worked...Occasionally you can do that—as a writer—*Homicide* did it on their final episode. And sometimes they get away with it on *L.A. Law*...just stop, forget the plot and let the people talk a little. I also see stuff on *Northern Exposure* that is delightful. It's just chatter. They're sexually attracted. He's angry at her. She's angry at him and the story stops and the people emerge. It's kind of a French approach, the French do that a lot. You see it in independent films—*The Crying Game*, of course, but even in something as mainstream as *Unforgiven*.

These screenwriters struggled to explain how they worked to create believable characters, growing frustrated when their words failed even them. Despite one writer's efforts at clarity, the creative process remained ineffable:

I can't answer that question because it comes to you while you are at the typewriter. You know you have a scene to do and it's got to move from A to B. So you write the scene and it just kind of lies there and you do it again and it lies there and you say, "there's something wrong with it," and suddenly you get an idea to try something that's just very offbeat, the character behaves in a totally opposite way and suddenly it comes to life. And then you go about making that believable, setting up the forces that make that character behave in that way. And then the character becomes interesting. But it's a conditioned instinct you acquire after years of doing it...

Another writer outlined his experience developing what he considered "unique" characters:

...you start with something unusual to begin with, like a screenplay I did. There's a homeless person sleeping in an alley and they recruit him to become a snitch for the police. And he turns out to be an extremely bright, sensitive guy who's fallen on bad times and becomes an alcoholic, but he's an amazingly deep and feeling human being. Well, you don't expect that and he withholds that and little by little...he becomes a wonderful character. I mean, there is a whole life in that little vignette...and those are some of the things you can do if you really like dealing with human beings and you like people...in that area I have been successful and that works for me...I've been able to make people come alive and that's important for me.

It was not uncommon to hear writers describe their affection for their creations. "I'm working on this one character now," a writer revealed. "She's a woman dying of a neuro-muscular disease and I love her, I really love her. She has guts, determination, and she's not attractive, she's sort of working class, low rent. But I love her!"

Another writer rhapsodized over a television project he developed which garnered critical raves but ended up a ratings failure:

Now I produced that show the first season...And I took those characters that author had created and who were, in a sense—there was a lot of cardboard to them—even though they were interesting. The movie was excellent but the book itself had problems. So I went back to the book and got into the characters and I saw what I could do with it. And then when the series was made, I changed them and got much more into their pain and their sincerity and I tried to make it a realistic life and death situation...with every word you utter...you run the risk of...there goes your career, there goes your life, so—Oh Boy! Oh Boy!—it's very dangerous...it was not only intellectually valid because we did a tremendous amount of research on that, but it was exciting because we were dealing, underneath, with a life and death situation. I loved doing that show. It's not that way now, it's much more sentimental now.

It is clear that majority writers' personal experience informed their writing, contributing to their development of ideas and characters with which the audience could identify. Writers did not discuss any attempt to manipulate their own experience, making it acceptable to audiences or mass culture. However, this very process of manipulation may occur at an unconscious level. What is conscious and clear, however, is the importance of majority writers' personal stake in their work.

Art vs. Money

Certainly something other than creative drive motivated individuals to write for the Hollywood. Majority writers did not shy away from discussing the financial advantages to screenwriting. Most writers asserted that they worked in Hollywood to "make a living," "because it pays well," and because, as one individual tersely stated, "it's the only place where an average writer can make a killing." "Most of my work in Hollywood is the result of needing money," one writer explained. "You don't get inspiration very often...generally speaking, when you know you're getting to the end of the job and you're going to need money for the family, you say to yourself, I better sell something within the next 90 days or I am going to be in trouble."

The question of what motivated these writers generated more complex answers than I originally imagined. Asking screenwriters if they worked for artistic fulfillment or money proved meaningless. Indeed, one writer insisted, "screenwriting is not an art, it's more of a craft. Money is the only reason to do it." However, many writers also stated they could not write simply for money. One writer was emphatic that he had to develop feelings for the material, that the drive to write had to proceed beyond financial need. "Well, once you get into it, unless you develop that feeling for yourself, it doesn't work," he claimed. "I forget about the money. I become deeply involved in the people and they become *my* people."

Another writer explained that there is always pressure in Hollywood to blend creative and professional concerns, even among the least likely of candidates. "Well, there is a TV producer who's famous," the writer began. "I mean he's the schlock master of television—Aaron Spelling. But Aaron Spelling...is very sensitive to the fact that he makes shit and he'll always say, 'Well, I know it's not *Family*.' *Family* was his one show he's proud of. He says that over and over again: 'I know it's not *Family* but *90210* entertains people.'"

It is true that screenwriters worked for the money. They also added that they wrote for personal satisfaction and the power of having their effort shared with an extensive audience. However, in examining their responses more closely, majority writers divided into two distinct groups. First, there were the individuals who worked to support a "habit." Their desire for money brought them to Hollywood although they consider themselves "primarily" playwrights, poets, or novelists. While their "serious" writing rarely brought financial security, screenwriting allowed these individuals to support themselves and their families when their other work could not. "I'm not really a screen-writer," one individual explained, "my background is as a journalist—I guess I still think of myself as a journalist. I'm working on a non-fiction book right now that's very important to me. I do screenplays on the side. It's certainly not my *raison d'être*."

Most Anglo writers issued disclaimers, insisting that working as screenwriters did not constitute their major professional commitment. These writers downplayed their identification with Hollywood, attempting to dissociate themselves from the industry as clearly as possible. When not detailing their other projects (e.g., books, articles, plays), these writers vehemently denied any interest in Hollywood beyond the financial.

A second group of writers viewed Hollywood as an end in itself, working in the industry as their calling. Many described plans to someday produce, direct, or call the shots as industry moguls. Screenwriting is perceived as the first step in establishing their positions. "I really don't care right now," a young screenwriter explained. "I mean it's nice to make that kind of money if they're stupid enough to pay me. [laughter] But I don't really care about that or the writing. What I really want to do is get to direct and this is the fastest way to do it." Another writer echoed these same wishes:

I write because I want to grow up and be a director. You know, it's like the joke. Mother Theresa dies and, goes to heaven and God says to her, "What do you want, as a reward for all your hard work, my child? You have done so much for others. What do *you* want?" And she answers, "I want to direct." I think that's pretty much how everyone feels.

Armed with either of these approaches, writers defended themselves against the frustration of being taken for granted. If work served as a stepping stone to their real desires, whether inside or outside of Hollywood, the misery could only be temporary. It was a sacrifice made in the present, for rewards in the future. All of this backfired when writers became trapped working full-time in Hollywood, unable to advance in the industry and too dependent on their earnings to leave. These men expressed the greatest ambivalence over their work in Hollywood. One writer explained:

Screenwriting sort of make you lose part of your respect for yourself. You have to keep everything in proportion. But it's hard. And everyone has their price, even nice Jewish boys from the Bronx. You have to remember not to take yourself too seriously.

Of course, for these white, male majority writers, there was always the consolation of the paycheck. This consolation proved necessary when each man was faced with the loss of creative control.

Control

Although the script may be theirs to begin with, writers exert little control over the ultimate shape of their work. This reality informs their accomplishment and fuels their dissatisfaction. Majority writers expressed regret at being routinely denied the satisfaction of seeing their creative efforts reach the screen intact. "Intellectually I know, I have to let go of the material," one writer stated, "That's part of the rules of the game. It's just that thinking about it is one thing but having it actually happen to you is another. You think you can deal with it but it's frustrating."

Majority writers all expressed feelings of possessiveness concerning their creations, but worked to overcome these emotions. "Once it's sold, it's gone and you've just got to let it go," another writer explained. "There's no two ways about it. It's not yours anymore. Whatever they want to do to it, they can and they will—you can bet on it. Don't think anyone will save parts of your screenplay because they think it's 'good.' You've got to kiss it goodbye. And go on to the next project. Otherwise you're dead. And you don't belong in this line of work."

Once sold, scripts are often rewritten, irrespective of quality. In many cases, according to writers, such rewrites do more harm than good. Rewrites may have little to do with script quality, but instead satisfy the various agendas of individuals involved with the film. "They say be creative and do whatever you want," one writer claimed, "then when we do that, they want to hack it up so it will be marketable. In movies and in TV they have all these ideas about what the audience wants to see and what the demographics are and what marketing surveys tell them. And they don't know a fucking thing. And they take their ignorance out on the script."

Many majority writers complained that their scripts were unrecognizable in their final form. One writer described a screenplay that "started out as an action adventure pirate story. There was probably one female character in my screenplay and she was dressed up as a boy—she stowed away on ship. By the time it was filmed it was your basic 'tits and ass' jiggle story that just happened to take place on board a ship. But it wasn't about pirates and it wasn't about adventure. It was about getting the audience titillated by a sexual affair between the captain of the ship and a sort of female pirate."

Such revisions open up the problem of screen credits, with the Writers Guild arbitrating disputes. However, none of the writers interviewed reported any experience with screen credits arbitration. Instead, preoccupied with preserving the integrity of their work, they lamented what occurred when other individuals who were not writers tried to revise their screenplays.

Not one of the majority writers interviewed complained about revisions completed by other writers. Additionally, several majority writers discussed rewriting the work of others. One writer labeled himself a script doctor and claimed he rewrote screenplays from other writers more frequently than he wrote original screenplays himself. Having exchanged roles on various projects, both writing and revising, majority writers did not attack other writers. Instead, they reserved their enmity for executives, producers and directors. Older writers were more vocal in their outrage, offering a backlog of illustrative anecdotes. For example, one veteran screenwriter complained:

I don't care if it was even a "B" movie, the directors always feel they've got to interfere. All this auteur shit was hot and they all thought they were the makers of their own stories, the singers of their own songs and I'll tell you, it was frustrating. The directors who tried the most to "fix" scripts were always the ones who knew the least about writing. And they were utterly sure—even if they didn't say it—that they could do a better job. The only directors who understand, and there are a few of them, very, very few, are directors who have been writers. And even some of them, because they've been writers, insist they can do a better job.

Despite their resentment of their loss of control, none of the majority writers took their powerlessness personally. These men all viewed their lack of control as a function of the screenwriter's position in Hollywood. One writer portrayed this frustrating existence:

Now when you start, you go through the process of discussing the idea and they say "okay" and they make a deal with you to write the story and do the script. If you're a young writer they start with a story with an option for a screenplay, but with an experienced writer you make a deal for the whole thing right at the beginning then you write a story after a conference or two and they begin to put their input in...they say, "We like this, we like this, but you really can't do this, this guy isn't sympathetic, we gotta get him sympathetic." And you say, "This isn't really real to do that with this kind of character" and they say, "Well, that's the way we have to do it, can you find a way of doing that?" and you say, "Well, let me think about it," and finally you come up with a way of doing it and that's generally the process it goes through from beginning to end, they have input in this story, they get story revisions, they have another story revision, then there's a conference before you do your first draft, then you have input from the network or the studio and you do a second draft and you do revisions...and you're continually getting input from the network or the director or the studio and you really have to just sit there and listen because *if you argue and you're the least bit contentious they never use you again, you're too difficult to deal with, the conferences take too long and the people who work are the people who are extremely cooperative.*

Majority writers detailed the strategies they used for acquiring, maintaining, and surrendering control. Cooperation was central to these descriptions. Writers repeatedly stressed the importance of agreeableness and equanimity. A cooperative attitude was a necessity because, as one writer stated, "We are expendable. Dispensable, replaceable. If we don't go along with them, there are six thousand more where we came from. And there are six thousand more ready to take our place."

Successful majority writers adapted compromise as their primary strategy for survival in Hollywood. "You've got to know when to give in—which is most of the time," one writer sourly observed. Based on their experience in Hollywood, writers adopted additional strategies to maintain a pretense of control. Younger writers focused on future plans that included producing and directing or looking forward to projects "outside" of Hollywood. Such a future orientation helped less experienced screenwriters deal with immediate loss of control. One writer explained:

I know when I sell a script or a treatment, that's it, goodbye, it's gone. But I know that one day there'll be the one that I get to control, that I get to direct, and that'll be my baby. Until then, I really don't care. I'll do what they want me to do and I'll let them do whatever they want to my work. I'll jump through hoops. When I decide, though, that I'm going to do a script and hopefully I'll have the power to do it, no one will tell me what to do with it.

Older and more experienced writers claimed they emotionally detached themselves from the fate of their work. In certain cases, however, they exerted more control over favorite scripts when they served as producers, demanding such a position as part of their conditions of sale.

Based on previous commercial success, several writers had amassed enough power to function as producers or, better still, writer-producers. Ironically, these individuals soon discovered that while producers' responsibilities were immense, their actual authority was illusory. Few writers discussed producing films positively. Instead, most expressed disillusionment. According to one writer, the producer's role is a thankless one, lacking any real control. "I get a percentage of the profits as a writer anyway, so what's the big deal about hanging on as a producer?" he asked. "To protect my script? That has turned out to be a lot of bullshit anyway. And what kind of true respect do producers get from the media, the reviewers, the audiences? Forget it."

Despite writers' claims that producing afforded them little power, they continued functioning as producers, perhaps unwilling to surrender what control they had attained. Their desire to continue producing was couched largely in terms of negatives. Writers did not focus on what they could accomplish as producers. Instead, they concentrated on the problems they could avert. Their work was preventive rather than creative.

"I've written this script for a television movie and the network wants to do it," one writer remarked. "The only way it can get done at least halfway decently is if I produce it and what can I say? We'll be filming in Hawaii...and I can be there watching, making sure nothing gets fucked up."

When discussing their work as producers, writers' creative sensibilities evaporated. Instead, they focused on organization, budget, employment practices, and other business concerns. The producer's responsibilities existed completely opposite writers' concerns. Indeed, several majority writers complained that once they worked as producers, their productivity as writers suffered.

Production responsibilities often proved crushing. Writers, accustomed to solitary work, may be ill prepared for such tasks. In addition, functioning as a producer does not necessarily afford a writer more control. Majority writers appear to have negotiated an uneasy truce with Hollywood powers. Writers cooperate and compromise when they feel they have no choice, promising themselves eventual authority. Ultimate authority is exercised when the writer can produce *and* direct his own script, a rare occurrence. Not one of the majority writers interviewed had directed their own scripts, although several expressed the desire to do so in the future. These writers insisted that as directors they could make the type of films they wanted, although when pressed they admitted that directors may experience just as much powerlessness when beholden to "the suits" for money.

Culture-Makers

Beyond controlling the fate of their work and their position in Hollywood, how did these writers view their role in and impact on mass culture? Writers responded to the issues raised by this question by first offering their observations on the intersection of Hollywood and mass culture. Every majority writer commented about the deteriorating quality of modern intellectual life, often hypothesizing that Hollywood was partly responsible, fostering the lack of critical thinking exhibited by modern audiences. One writer explained:

You have all the violence oriented shows which, in my opinion, are damaging. I don't care what people say and what parents want their children to do or what they don't want them to do...people say it's a good safety valve—like pornography has some very healthy aspects to it—but I don't think violence does...you sometimes scan the tube in the evening looking for something and you go past gun-fire and wrecks and car chases and people with knives and bullets being fired. It's garbage. And that's being fed into the consumer's hunger for garbage. So the networks are at fault here, so are the studios—and the writers, producers, and directors are too. And the culture, I think, is being destroyed by this kind of thing. I think it's extremely damaging. It tells you that this is entertaining. This is what life is like. This is a way that you can amuse yourself in your home in the evening instead of reading a book, all of which has been discussed many, many times, but to me, it's palpable, it's discouraging, it's very negative to the culture...and you know now it's not fantasy, it's these so-called reality shows "COPS" and all that—it's scary.

Still, most writers expressed skepticism over how much Hollywood actually influenced attitudes and behaviors. "There is *no way* to discuss this issue," one writer angrily insisted. "It's impossible, in a way it's a non-issue, it's 'Which came first, the chicken or the egg?' But then again, I'm not sure that culture is relevant to Hollywood..." "Leave Hollywood alone—it's an entertainment machine—that's all," another writer maintained. "I know what I am talking about. Culture and our impact upon it is not important to the people who make movies or television, we don't think about it."

Another writer expressed uncertainty about the impact of the entertainment industry on modern culture:

In dealing with social issues, I think the networks are sincere, generally, in trying to deal with these things like AIDS and domestic violence and racial issues, but, I just don't know how much good it does. It probably does some good but it generally does good with the people who are already enlightened. I mean, you know, you and I—if we had a political discussion, I really wouldn't change your mind, you really wouldn't change my mind, but we'd have a relationship. And so in television or movies, you're not really changing people's minds unless the people are people whose minds can be changed easily anyway. But when you put the other stuff on, the violence and the gunshots, you're dealing with those people and reinforcing their mind-sets, the same way you're reinforcing the mind-set of a liberal who says, "Yeh, that's true, I really should pay more attention to that. They're right, it's a good show." But the kids in the hood are watching this stuff and getting other ideas. I really really believe that television and motion pictures have tremendous impact—depending on who and where you are.

Many writers eventually discussed Hollywood's potential role as a force in reaffirming or changing values, attitudes, and behaviors. "Movies and even television...there's got to be some meaning in the material, that's what makes it good," one writer observed. "That's what I think makes it good. I mean, unless you're doing a melodrama, unless you're doing *The Amy Fisher Story*—God help you—or something like that. But ultimately, in any other show or any movie, you come down to intimacy and trust and the old values and that does work. It's the only thing that really works, that really lasts, that lifts the good movies and the good television shows above the rest of the crap."

Similarly, another writer observed that Hollywood missed many opportunities to provide much needed influence. "We don't give a shit," he claimed, "and we should, we have that opportunity...I mean, where do you find today any real or clear or sincere good values? We're in trouble, in the media and out there in the audience. It seems to me that we, in Hollywood, ought to do something about it."

When questioned about their specific role as culture-makers, influencing the behaviors or beliefs of audiences, writers initially insisted that they wrote to entertain, never considering other consequences of their work. "If I write a murder mystery—and I have—I don't think about whether that's going to cause someone to knock off someone else," one writer contended. "The thought never enters my mind. I also never set things up and say, 'I know if I write this movie it is going to get some kid in South Central off drugs.' That's giving myself too much credit."

Screenwriters focused on the personal in their work, even when working on scripts with blatantly political themes. These writers reported the desire to expose the American collective to their experiences, reworking their personal lives to resonate with the audience, irrespective of differences in background, ethnicity, or outlook. Through their writing, they impressed their dreams, experiences, and visions on the public, influencing what people saw, not what they believed.

One writer had worked doctoring the screenplay for a feature film with a plot centering on a high profile social problem. "I didn't want to solve the problem," he insisted. "I didn't even want the audience paying a whole lot of attention to it. The movie was *not* a political message, it was a piece of entertainment. It was a story—that's all—a story about a guy with marital problems and financial debt, dissatisfied with his wife, trying to satisfy her demands and all that, something anybody could identify with."

Most screenwriters perceived themselves as individuals who magnified culture, enlarging and elaborating upon aspects of the American scene. One writer explained:

No matter what you do, it's screened very carefully by the network. They take out words, they change characters, they say this person isn't sympathetic, so on and so forth. So what you are really doing is keying into the culture and providing the culture with what the culture seems to want, and it seems to me that you're not influencing the culture as much as reinforcing what's already there. If the culture is violence-oriented, that's what they will supply. Now movies do that too, in a way. But with television, it's immediate and it's sensitive to that and that's what they give and that's what they make us do, so it's very, very unusual for someone to come up with a totally new concept, particularly in a series or in "Movies of the Week." You may occasionally do something offbeat because you do a classic, y'know, somebody might come in with "Anna Karenina" so those are the conditions under which you work.

Another writer stated that success in Hollywood is guaranteed by "knowing what people want and giving it to them. I've been a success and the studios love me because I have my finger firmly on the pulse of what the American public wants. I know what they want better than even they know what they want."

Still, not one individual viewed himself as passive or "under the influence" of American culture. Instead, approximately two thirds of the majority screenwriters interviewed ended up discussing how the entertainment industry in general and screenwriters in particular "make" American culture. Although initially writers denied such a relationship, many unwittingly reversed their positions in later remarks. Several screenwriters admitted to a tendency to develop something beyond plot and characters. One writer stated that "what you try to do, or what I try to do is whatever I can to make the show entertaining and moving and I think generally the good dramatic writers try to do that...you can reinforce the traditional human values, hoping to counterbalance this stuff that destroys them."

Several screenwriters connected their personal experience to their role as culture-makers. "I guess I influence people's ideas and their attitudes," one writer admitted. "Sooner or later, you get that chance to take something that happened to you and show how you got through it, or didn't get through it, or wish you had gotten through it and you can put it down on paper and someone else puts it on the screen and someone else might see it and realize, 'Hey, things are gonna work out for me too' or 'Maybe I better change what I'm doing, how I'm living before it's too late.'"

Another writer acknowledged that a current project could potentially affect viewers watching:

I went in to a pitch a couple of ideas to a producer and right off the top she said, "Geez, I love that, we're really interested in that idea." Now the idea is that over-the-counter drugs can be very dangerous if you don't read the labels carefully or if you disregard the labels or you don't know what's supposed to be on the labels. See, sometimes the drug companies omit things in the labels and the drugs look innocuous and turn out to be innocuous unless they are taken in combination with another drug, then you have a very bad result. So that's the subject and they've been wanting to do that. Well, that's very helpful to the culture. There is a warning there and a subject matter that they are dealing with in a more or less responsible way.

Several screenwriters recalled scripts they had worked on that offered a message or a moral to the viewing audience. While communicating such meaning may not have been their primary motivation for writing, writers viewed such messages as an added benefit or an auxiliary feature of their trade. Certainly, making a case for the beneficial aspects of modern entertainment may serve as a a glib rationalization for commercial success. Nonetheless, these majority writers, for whatever reasons, felt compelled to repeatedly admit or "confess" that their screenplays communicated messages they considered significant. The degree to which this was done and the emphasis the message received depended on several factors, including writer status and screenplay content.

Several writers addressed the problem of how their work could impact culture negatively, portraying themselves as considering screenplay content carefully. However, their colleagues were not exempt from criticism. One writer found fault with one much-lauded feature film on child abuse, *This Boy's Life*, explaining:

It's the way they handle it that I object to...the way script dealt with abuse reminded me of *Something About Amelia*, which was years ago which I found kind of shocking, everybody was so pleasant in it—it seemed almost like a valentine, even though there was personal agony in the whole thing, it seemed totally unrealistic to me...and it wasn't real because in general the mother is complicitous in this relationship. The mother knows that there's incest going on and it's very complex...none of that was dealt with in that movie—just like they didn't deal with all the issues in the DeNiro movie and in that sense, you're doing the public a disservice, you're giving them incorrect information and that's no good, that's damaging.

When asked to describe writing projects they might find objectionable, majority writers' responses were nebulous, unfocused, and general. Screenwriters did not specify any topic as objectionable, instead mentioning projects involving "betrayal," "dishonesty," or "cruelty" as being antithetical to their personal values and creative abilities. "I can't do really hard pornography, anything that portrays an Arab in a good light—I have that knee-jerk bias against Arabs—and anything that portrays a black in a bad light," one writer succinctly stated.

Another veteran screenwriter regretted several scripts he had worked on for episodic television:

When I was first getting started...I worked only on shows that I liked. But there were occasionally times when I needed money very badly and I had to do shows that I loathed. I don't want to tell you the name of one of them. I really hated that show because some of the police were really frauds. One guy, of course was an undercover cop masquerading as a bad guy, he infiltrated certain areas and then turned on everyone, he was a snob about the police and saw himself as elite...It was hard for me to relate to him in any valid human way, to either what he was doing or the people he was dealing with. I just couldn't get with the show. I ended up selling only one script to them and it didn't turn out well. They wanted something funny and I got too heavy handed.

Another writer echoed these sentiments. "I once worked on a script that involved ideas I found very, very objectionable. It wasn't so much the theme of the script but the way there was a violence, a lot of evil—and the hero was involved. Well, I tried to come up with a story that I could handle and the producers liked the idea very much, but then when I did the script, the script did not turn out well, I didn't feel what I was doing and so it seemed mechanical and uninspired. The worst of it was, the characters just weren't real."

Several screenwriters mentioned their inability to create objectionable characters. "I rarely write people who are bad," one writer commented. "I write people who are wrong and who have taken wrong turns and defend those wrong turns, but they have a rationale and they are reachable. I can't write a totally gone person. I've met them but I can't...I guess that says something about my general view of human nature...no one is completely gone, completely bad."

Their personal reputations also figured in these writers' works. "Be careful what you write about," one writer, a veteran script "doctor" warned. "Even if there have been ten other writers on the script before you, once you run the paper through your own typewriter—metaphorically—it becomes yours. There are certain ideas and certain images I don't want my name associated with—and I don't care if I'm just fixing something on the script, like the dialogue, I won't do it."

Hollywood majority writers acknowledged their role as culture-makers unwillingly, initially denying their impact on the public. Despite their misgivings, ultimately screenwriters acknowledged their role as possible influences. Not all agreed that they "make" culture, however most saw themselves as actively, if not manufacturing at least influencing, culture. Part of writers' inability to see themselves as culture-makers can be traced to their lack of control in Hollywood. These writers may wonder how they could claim any influence/power over culture, when they fail to even control the outcome of their projects in Hollywood. Their impact on culture has little to do with their inadequacy inside Hollywood. Despite their second-class status, they belong to an enterprise whose impact on mass culture is profound.

Despite their ambivalence towards Hollywood, the screenwriters interviewed expressed the desire to continue working in the entertainment industry. In discussing the future, all writers mentioned the importance of increased control over their work. However, financial security, awards, and recognition went unmentioned as major goals.

More than anything, majority writers evidenced a great deal of pragmatism in their ambitions. No one expressed the wish to write a script that would alter culture or transform world politics. Writers made broad statements that both the mass media and the world were deteriorating and needed improvement. They linked this need with the media's potential power to facilitate change. But there were no specifics. When questioned about their own contributions to such change, writers stated that they wished to create "quality work," but failed to elaborate. The exact meaning of "quality" remains undefined.

There was no discussion of the general future of writers in Hollywood. Majority screenwriters expressed anxiety over their continued employment and access to Hollywood. Their future in Hollywood was always uncertain. But despite the vicissitudes of the industry, most writers were filled with personal plans and aspirations. "We give people their dreams," one writer maintained. "I hope Hollywood will let me fulfill mine."

Chapter Five

✦ ✦ ✦

Minority Writers

I've always known since I was nine years old that I wanted to be in this business as a writer. I was very fortunate. I grew up in Hollywood circumstances because my mother worked as the personal maid to Hollywood people and they encouraged me back then, a long time ago, when to be black and want to get into Hollywood—well, it was like you were being crazy, maybe it still is. So I finished high school and went to USC and got a degree in television and cinema and the day after I finished school I started as a page at NBC. I worked as a page in the mailroom, in the music department, and then in the program department...Then I worked my way up to becoming vice-president of community television, program development, and then current programming. In 1976 I left to go to Universal as a writer-producer. I produced, directed, and developed several series, movies for television and then in 1980 I went on my own, wrote a couple of movies, then in 1988 I came to where I am now senior vice president, production. And what my job is, is to develop and supervise movies from the inception of an idea all the way through till they're in the theaters. Basically, that's the story of my life. I made it, but it's been difficult, extremely difficult.

This writer's experience was not unique. Most minority writers expressed a "life long" passion for the movies and television, frequently claiming they made decisions early in life to "someday" work in Hollywood. However, despite their preoccupation, minority writers demonstrated—and described—a sense of distance from the workings of the industry.[1]

The reality of minority writers in Hollywood is characterized by distance. Their frustrations, successes and failures are all intensified by their status as outsiders, separate from the Hollywood mainstream. They have been allotted minimal attention in the literature on the entertainment industry. What little has been written about minorities in

69

Hollywood has focused on actors and celebrities. Although, there is a growing body of literature on women in the film industry, overall interest in minorities has been superficial and transitory. People of color have been neglected altogether.

Their outsider status is reinforced in today's Hollywood. Already undervalued as screenwriters, many claim they face additional obstacles due to their minority status. "It's a cliché, I know," one writer reflected, "but I always feel like I'm on the outside looking in."

These writers did not always feel like outsiders. Most recalled upbringings marked by familial love and academic achievement that nurtured their self-esteem and initiative. "From an early age," one writer recalled, "I believed I could do anything I wanted to do." In general, minority writers described similar backgrounds, often revealing a childhood interest in writing that continued into adulthood. "I started writing at an early age," one African-American woman remembered. "When I got out of graduate school I didn't do any screenwriting immediately but I was writing other things, always writing. I am a poet and I wrote and published a book and wrote a couple of plays back then and the writing wanted to come through on an everyday continual basis so I gave up film editing and started writing professionally in 1980." This writer earned a bachelor's degree in English, an M.F.A. from Columbia University and proceeded to work as a film editor. Her university education and professional experience were typical of most minority writers.

As a group, minority writers were considerably younger than their majority counterparts. All reported completing undergraduate degrees, with over half the individuals interviewed attending some type of film program or film school, either at a university or under the auspices of the American Film Institute. However, with their education over, many minority writers reported great difficulties in gaining access to Hollywood. While access to the industry constituted a dilemma for all screenwriters, for minorities, it was a particularly frustrating struggle, arousing strong emotional reactions. Their sense of distance from Hollywood made the process of "breaking in" to Hollywood extremely troublesome for most minority writers.

Geography was yet another measure of minority writers' separation from the entertainment industry. Several lived far from Hollywood and the west side, in communities south or east of Los Angeles. Even relatively successful writers maintained homes in these outlying areas, although the four most well-known minority writers lived in the West Los Angeles area, home to many industry principals. Still, minority writers' overall geographic remoteness reinforced their detachment from the industry mainstream.

This distance from Hollywood also translated to minority writers' private lives. Most majority writers, whatever their level of success, offered insider information and Hollywood gossip. They frequented clubs, restaurants, and recreational facilities popular among the Hollywood elite, participating in the informal culture of Hollywood. Minority writers neither claimed insider status nor reported similar experiences. This difference emerged even when arranging interviews. Majority writers selected locations frequented by the Hollywood establishment, enabling them to increase their visibility. Ethnic minority writers rarely suggested such places, often waiting until I recommended where to meet. The exceptions were the women writers who matched majority writers in selecting locales popular among the industry establishment.

By labeling themselves "minorities," these writers reinforced their separate status, further distancing themselves from the industry structure. With two exceptions,[2] these men and women explicitly described themselves as "minority writers" or "people of color." They defined their relationship to American majority culture and to Hollywood primarily in terms of their minority status. These individuals discussed their unique position in Hollywood; even writers who had achieved success and acceptance expressed a sense of being "different."

These writers' identification with their minority status emerged as they related creative and personal concerns. They described how their minority identities influenced what they wrote about as well as their experiences in the industry. For those who belonged to more than one minority group, race or ethnicity superseded all other statuses. While others might label them differently, these writers' primary identities involved ethnicity. One writer explained:

I think what I most identify now as my cultural background is Latino. My folks, my family, where I was raised, my high school, is all Latino and at that time I was not disabled, so the real conditioned responses of my life are very Latino. The macho image...affected my acceptance of the disability...I got involved in the "Chicano" movement, everything was to me Latino. But then I found out that within the Latino community, I was still disabled...then I started seeing other people look at me as a disabled individual within another group. This happened with the entertainment industry. I think that most people...when they first see me, deal with me as a disabled person, then Latino.

Other writers adamantly claimed that race or ethnicity took precedence, not only in their self-conceptualization, but in terms of how others defined them. One African-American writer discussed how she never felt she belonged in Hollywood women's organizations:

Most of the women that were in "Women in Film" had no sensitivity to my problems as a black woman. I mean, they had sensitivity as being women, but not black...a lot of time I would see them at the Melting Pot [restaurant] or Farmers Market...they never recognized me, never spoke to me and I felt like saying, "Come on!!" I was the *only* black woman at the meetings and the only one of eight women at the Directors Guild and here they would walk right past me. But that convinced me, although I am a woman writer, I am first of all an African-American woman writer.

The minority identification of these writers coupled with their sense of separation affected their responses to the industry. Minority writers varied in their ability to understand Hollywood, either intuitively or through experience. Some offered astute observations while others displayed a surprising lack of knowledge. Writers who possessed a "sense" of Hollywood, often revealed their understanding in subtle ways, casually using correct or little known terminology, peppering their conversation with Yiddish phrases.[3] Beyond vocabulary, these writers accurately described the transitory and strategic nature of relationships in the industry. One female writer experienced overnight celebrity from the critical and commercial acclaim her first screenplay received, including an Academy Award nomination. Still, she remained philosophical about her success. "I know why my phone is ringing and why I have so many friends," she mused. "Right now I am the flavor of the month and next month it's all going to change. Her evaluation proved correct as she encountered difficulties acquiring a producer and financial backing for her next project. In another writer's case, while his initial success has been sustained, he still evinced a wary, somewhat cynical attitude towards personal interactions in the industry, claiming:

Your agents are only going to send you to people who like your work. He sends it out to ten people, five will call back and say, "Well, I want to meet this guy," so you only meet people who like it...it went to my head for little while and then two years later I had been through this and I had friends just starting out, going to meetings, they are hearing the same things I heard, making them excited. I don't know whether or not they are already a little more cynical than I was. It [the cynicism] comes fast after a couple of weeks, you know, it's just like a handshake they have to do, with producers overpraising...everything is the greatest. You're always the greatest and they always want you—if not this project then the next one: "We'll do something together." They say that to everybody.

Approximately one-third of the minority writers interviewed demonstrated a fundamental Hollywood "sense," attuned to the inner workings of the entertainment industry. Their remarks resembled those made by majority writers as well as Hollywood producers and executives. While such a "sense" of Hollywood did not guarantee access or success, the busiest minority writers all demonstrated an ability to translate their understanding into action. They comprehended the Hollywood structure and accepted its rituals of overpraise and broken promises, philosophically. "You are still going to be disappointed and there are things that you going to hate," one writer explained, "but you look at this business realistically."

These writers viewed Hollywood as a profit-making enterprise. "Nine out of ten of these people will sell their mother for a hit," one writer succinctly stated. "I did research on the early days of Hollywood," a female screenwriter commented, "and realized it was exactly the same then as it is now. It's not different at all. The ratio of business to creativity is exactly the same—and business wins out. Now the corporate world may be taking over but it doesn't matter, business was a priority before they got there. All this bullshit about 'The Year of the Woman' is a lot of propaganda. It's the year of the dollar, just like it is every year." An African-American writer offered an elaborate metaphor:

One night I woke up at 1:00 a.m...and I was staring at my ceiling and I just said, "I wonder how do you work in Hollywood?" And it's almost like this voice gave me this answer: "Working in Hollywood is like trying to get a three-headed monster to eat out of your hand." So then I asked, "How do you get a three-headed monster to eat out of your hand?" Well, first you define the heads of the monster. The first head of the monster is the spirit of money and that's represented by ratings, producers and all the pressures that time and money create. So that's head number one...Head number two is the creative muse, the one who has all the ideas, all the stories, the one I am probably most familiar with, most comfortable with, you have to have her always on your side because otherwise, what are you going to write? The third head has a zillion eyes and one big mouth and that's the audience who are hungrier than they are discerning.

This writer explained that to succeed, she would have to satisfy all three "heads" of the Hollywood monster. However, many minority writers did not understand the mechanics of the entertainment industry—with or without the use of such intricate metaphors.

It was unclear why a sense of Hollywood has eluded the remaining minority screenwriters. These individuals ignored the collaborative nature of the industry, concentrating instead on screenwriting alone. While they understood particular facets of industry structure, they were unable to construct a coherent picture of Hollywood's operation, missing even basic points. Ultimately, it is unclear where the confusion began: with an inadequate knowledge of Hollywood leading to a lack of access or blocked access resulting in an impaired understanding of the industry.

There were additional misunderstandings. Minority conceptualizations of Hollywood often assumed a moralistic tone. While trying to avoid appearing judgmental, disapproval was often implicit or even explicit in their observations of the industry. "It occurred to me that people in Hollywood are not nice," one female writer opined. "It's a way in which you pride yourself on being better than everybody else. I mean you get a whole bunch of people that feel that they have to be better than everybody else...this doesn't make for nice people. The priority in Hollywood is not about niceness, in fact, niceness is something to be looked down upon."

Another African-American writer brought up the problem of trust. "There is a lot of pretentiousness in this town," she explained. "There are very few people you can trust. Like the way I am sitting here talking to you. If I sat here and talked to someone in the industry like this, you never know what they are going to go and do with the information. And that's draining on you. After awhile, it is very draining that you can't have anybody that you can talk to and trust them, they're concerned with how they're going to look."

This theme of pretentiousness surfaced repeatedly in minority writers' remarks. The image of Hollywood's white writers, producers, and executives invoked most often involved Bel-Air addresses and foreign luxury cars. Six minority writers, all with differing backgrounds, offered identical views of the industry establishment. One writer stated that, "these guys sit up in their houses in Bel-Air in their insulated environments, driving their Mercedes—air-conditioned Mercedes no less—to and from the studios where they get no input, no sense-stimulation from anything other than the environment that they have been accustomed to." Another writer concurred that "what they see has become muted by the lives they lead which are sort of somewhere between the Mercedes, the pool, and the office." And again, a Latino writer saw majority writers as "sitting in a pillbox on the lot and going back to Bel-Air and sleeping and coming back to the pillbox."

One African-American writer took exception to the cliché of Hollywood affluence used by many minority writers to characterize the industry. "They think everybody out here is driving a Mercedes, drinking high class stuff and wearing Hawaiian shirts and Gucci shoes and going to great sex orgies and taking dope," he commented, "but it's an industry in which...the real stories show, it's a lot of hard work. It's chancy, you can be up one day and down the next. It's not as easy as it looks. People don't party hard, they work."

Still, two-thirds of the minority writers interviewed saw Hollywood as peopled by uncaring, hedonistic white writers, producers, and executives, creatively bankrupt and closed to new ideas, particularly those offered by minorities. But while they pointed an accusing finger at the system, minority writers did not specify their consequent plans or creative actions. Viewing Hollywood as an adversary, their ideas deteriorated into complaints against the system rather than guides to action. These writers differed from the individuals who comprehended the dynamics of the industry and planned their endeavors accordingly.

Culture-Makers

To a greater extent than majority writers minorities viewed the entertainment industry as a powerful force in mass culture. "I think it's a major subject as to how Hollywood influences the culture...around the world. There is nothing more powerful," one female writer insisted. "I would argue that you are far more powerful sitting in an office in Hollywood making movies than you are sitting in the U.S. Congress.

You have far more power over...how people in the world think in the long run."

"There will always be films influencing society," a Latino writer claimed, "because if you look at certain films, they have influenced the way people dress, if you look at certain films, they have influenced the way people think and public opinion. I think that when you have a film and you see somebody up there, 30 or 40 feet high, acting a certain way, you are going to have people go and act in a certain way. Look at something like *Falling Down*. I hate to think what that did to people in L.A. during the Rodney King trials.

An African-American screenwriter discussed the "sociocultural possibilities of film and what could be done to change society vis-à-vis film." Other minority writers shared his view that culture and social organization could be transformed with the mass media serving as the catalyst for change. A female writer explained, "The reason I entered movies was that it had such a potential to raise consciousness, to make people feel, to make people angry, to make people say, 'God I do that but I don't want to do that anymore,' and to reflect so many of the wonderful and horrible things about human nature."

Not all minority writers agreed on the culture-making capacity of Hollywood. Three writers insisted that Hollywood reflected culture. One Latino writer asserted that the networks waited until a social problem was "safe" or acceptable and then produced the perfunctory television-movie with attendant publicity. Rather than heralding change, she viewed television as reflecting what had already happened in society:

All of those different issues which I think most people are very much aware of today, Hollywood seems to back away and wait until the particular social issue becomes the kind of chic interest and all of a sudden, whether it's the *National Enquirer* or *Time Magazine* or *NBC News*...all of a sudden when you are getting blitzed and bombarded by all of those different things, *then* the industry says, "Okay, now we are going to address child abuse, now we are going to address this..." So in a way, they are playing it safe and they are the reflectors of a social problem...here they have the perfect opportunity to educate, to dispel myths, to give solutions to problems which they have decided not to really deal with. What a waste!

Still, this attitude was not prevalent among minority writers. "I think in its greatest moments, Hollywood can challenge and it can lead—it can send people in the right direction," one black writer insisted. "In terms of commercial television, it probably doesn't happen often enough, but there have been some really great moments on television that did serve, I think, to move this society forward. And look at something like *In Living Color.*"

Several minority writers insisted that the entertainment industry underestimated or altogether ignored its impact on viewers. "They don't think their impact is that great," one female writer claimed. "They feel that children and adults distinguish that there is a piece of glass or screen between them and what they are seeing—whether it's violence or anti-social behavior, consumption of strange foods or promiscuous sex, or whatever the problems are—that it's not really affecting kids."

While emphasizing its impact, minority writers blamed the industry for abusing its power, holding Hollywood accountable for perpetuating stereotypes and ideas that were "troubling." Several individuals contended that the entertainment industry was partly responsible for worsening both the image and actual status of minority groups. And, despite their sense of separation from Hollywood, minority writers probed their own role in culture-making: influencing attitudes and behavior.

Certain writers specified what they hoped to communicate in their writing as well as what they hoped to avoid. "I wanted to change a lot of attitudes," a disabled writer explained, "in this script [about disabled individuals]. There is not a promising young athlete whose life has been cut short...it's just normal people, dealing with normal problems of getting along and a lot of details that people don't know about...I want to educate the audience with this script."

The idea of "educating" or enlightening audiences emerged as a frequent theme. Two-thirds of the writers interviewed mentioned a wish to alter public perceptions in some way. One woman writer remarked, "I would like them to think a script is clever, that there is some kind of edge to it, that they see it as something that's got significance...but a script can only be enlightening in a sense that one can glimpse some view of something that maybe one didn't understand before and it humanizes it." Another writer commented, "I know doing TV is not high status, but I don't care about that. Someone might say it's small time, but I do enjoy my work. And no matter what it is, I'll try to do some consciousness raising."

Several writers specified messages conveyed by their stories. One, discussing a project based loosely on the life of singer Tina Turner, remarked, "If I have one issue to focus on that's worthwhile in that script, then it's the question of women and what...the women's movement did. Of course, I am not going to face this head on—you don't see her [Tina Turner] going to a NOW meeting, but those are the issues that are in the script and I can latch on to them."

A few writers stressed appropriateness, outlining the dangers of indiscriminately placing messages in scripts. "I think you really have to choose the instance carefully," one African-American woman warned. "There are a lot of times when people—and maybe they're very well-meaning people—try to do something with their work that's going to have sociological impact...and if it's not done absolutely right, it's very offensive."

Another writer was even more emphatic when he explained, "I don't believe that people are going to get the message if they are not ready for it. I think that if people are made to feel good, if they are entertained, they will get the message."

For some writers, screenwriting was rarely the correct venue for communicating ideas in any form. "You aren't there to make statements or send messages," one writer commented. "There's always problems. What's more important, the messages or the joke? The art is to have them combined but...you never sacrifice the joke for the message." Another writer was even more direct. "The messages are not that important," he began, "because there's a lot of great messages out there but the world is still a piece of shit. I mean, that's reality." One Latino writer explained:

Luis Valdez has worked very hard and won a lot of awards and where is he today? He still needed an executive producer to do *La Bamba* to godfather the movie and he only had a small budget. We are not talking about doing a ten million dollar picture. This was maybe a two to three million dollar picture. And now he can't get the movie about Frida Kahlo off the ground. So with all the messages and all of this—the little picture still disappeared into the woodwork. I think if you get the financial security afforded by a big commercial success, then you can make all the message pictures you want.

Certain individuals tried to combine the goals of entertaining and enlightening audiences. "Entertainment is number one," a writer remarked. "Just look at TV and what's great on TV and even though Bill Cosby did messages in his thing, or Roseanne does messages in her show, they're very subtle or they're laced with humor." The place of messages in their screenwriting endeavors divided minority opinion although most individuals communicated ideas in at least part of their work.

In addition to messages they sought to communicate, there were topics minority writers wished to avoid. Like majority writers, minority individuals described objectionable topics and script assignments they would reject. Their responses focused on minority stereotyping as well as more general concerns.

Many writers discussed their resistance to working on scripts about minority groups outside their own. One black female writer, struggling with the issue, admitted:

There are probably certain cultures that I don't understand and someone from that culture should be in there writing it. Years ago I had a big problem with *The Color Purple*—with the writer and the director...there was something about Steven Spielberg and I *am* going to say it—he does not understand black culture and he shouldn't have directed it and they had to go all the way over to Scandinavia to get some guy to write about black culture and there are not enough black writers here? I don't think so. And he [the screenwriter] does not understand African-American culture either.

Many writers expressed concern over the portrayal of cultural groups. They approached material more globally than writers who objected to specific characterizations. One African-American writer explained:

As an example, just an extreme example, if somebody wanted me to write something which was really negative about black folks, for that matter, about anyone, I don't think I could do it. I don't think I could write a story that is negative about women or Japanese or something if it wasn't true and I really knew it wasn't true...I mean there are negative characters and negative individuals...there are people like that, that exist, but whenever you start portraying a whole segment of society as something negative, then I know I wouldn't want to be involved in something like that.

Another writer evinced a similar attitude when he explained, "I can understand why a picture like *Falling Down* can be successful as well as some other pictures of that nature, but I personally would not allow myself to write that way or to...portray people in that fashion, not as a whole group anyway. I could not say, "All these Greeks are this way," or "All these Italians are this way," or "All these Puerto Ricans are this way."

Some minority writers limited their objections to stylistic concerns, relating that they could not accept certain projects because of creative constraints. "I really find a lot of reality television objectionable," one Latino writer stated, while another African-American writer discussed her resistance to writing scripts that featured insult comedy, explaining that humor evolving from character development was "a lot nicer to write." Another black writer concurred with this view, explaining, "I don't like cruel comedy...I don't like racial or sexual slurs. A lot of shows come up with that...I'd rather look for a good story." Still, many writers objected to formats they were forced to accommodate working on episodic television, problems that embraced creative concerns rather than value issues.

Slightly more than half the minority writers specified topics they found objectionable. One writer insisted, "There are two things I can't write about. I can't write about child abuse and I can't write about rape. There's just something about children being helpless...and being victimized by adults who use their cunning, use their conniving ways to convince a child to do what they want them to do...I can't write that kind of story. I don't write 'jiggle stories,' I don't do *Sandlot*, although that garbage makes a lot of money, if you're good at writing garbage. I write what I like to write."

A few individuals discussed violence. One disabled writer flatly stated, "I wouldn't write a slasher film, I couldn't." Similarly, a woman writer commented, "I could not write something like *Texas Chainsaw Massacre* because it simply demeans humanity. Life is cheap in a piece like that."

Still, not every individual ruled out violent subject matter. One black writer carefully explained that she "had no problem with violence but it's got to be hot blooded violence and not cold blooded violence. People get hurt and people do things that can destroy things...my writing is not without violence, it's not without confrontation but in my work, if somebody dies, it will be somebody you have cared about, it won't be just an extra...I wrote a violent scene...it wasn't just your stock car chase and it wasn't a fight, it was people going down in a hail of passion."

Minority descriptions of objectionable topics were generally both political and personal. One screenwriter insisted that "You make a commitment to yourself that you're not interested in writing films that are sexist, that are racist, that are exploitive. You make a decision that you are not going to make exploitive films."

The views of Hollywood offered by minority writers varied. However one element remained strangely absent from their discussions: money. While Hollywood was depicted as a business, preoccupied with profit and financial gain, writers did not reveal any substantial personal interest in moneymaking.

Art vs. Money

While majority writers openly acknowledged their financial stake in screenwriting, such admissions were altogether absent from minority writers' comments. "Well, I think probably more than anything else the things that attracted me to Hollywood were the glamour and the creative possibilities," one black male writer related. "I mean, there is a lot of money to be made, but I am more interested in writing than in anything else. I wanted to write for television and movies." His response typified the lack of interest in money exhibited by most minority writers.

Aside from three women writers who mentioned how economic necessity following divorce spurred their decision to work, financial security was underemphasized by minority writers. Several individuals were both cautious and cautionary about overinvolvement with material gain, invoking the negative image of the majority writer living in Bel-Air, driving a Mercedes, lunching at The Ivy. "If all your concerns are just making money and getting another show on the network and you spend all your time doing that...you'll get stale and your work will be nothing," one writer admonished. A Latino writer maintained, "It is a lot easier selling out, but I don't think it's a good thing. I think it puts you in a Procrustean bed and they cut off your head and your feet and you all fit the same mold or they stretch you out and you tend to be clones without any kind of soul."

One writer specifically discussed the lack of commercial appeal predicted for a feature film produced from his original screenplay. "It's about ugly people and a very sick, pessimistic world and there is no redemption...I know it's not going to be financially successful," he admitted, "but that's not really important to me."

His attitude was echoed by most minority writers, particularly those dedicated to communicating the minority experience to audiences. "We aren't interested in making Doris Day movies, we aren't interested in writing those kind of stories," one writer explained. "We want to talk about our stories. We never worried about making money. I work more for the love and advancement of cinema art and also to speak directly to our communities. It's not really a question of money because most of us came from generally working-class families and we never really had a concept of money, really. So it wasn't the question of money at all, or even prestige."

"It's not that we want to make money so we need an audience," another minority writer commented. "Instead, we felt that we have something to say so we need an audience."

Despite their apparent lack of interest in money, several minority writers commented on the relationship between money and art in Hollywood. These writers dismissed the art vs. business dichotomy as irrelevant because, as one woman insisted, "Just by sheer numbers, in terms of money, you've got to become a business man...at the same time you're an artist." An African-American woman observed:

I think I have a very good slant on how the business works...I think TV and film are the children of a very stormy marriage between business and art. They need each other. The businessman needs the shows to fill in the spaces between commercials and the artists need the businessmen to pay for it, support it, and so there is always bickering, but they have to stick together for the sake of the children. Now, that's one way I have of looking at it—that's my big picture.

Indeed, as a group, minority writers held themselves "above" the sensibilities of Hollywood: while the industry establishment worried exclusively about profit, minorities were concerned with communication. This distinction intensified the sense of distance minority writers already experienced. Money is important in Hollywood, but these writers seemed to be saying it just does not matter to them. While moneymaking and material success did not dominate minority discussions, acceptance by the Hollywood establishment did.

Unlike majority writers, minority individuals did not talk about their professional efforts outside the industry. While a few writers mentioned working on plays, there was little substantive discussion of writing unrelated to Hollywood. Most of these writers claimed they did not envision a professional life outside of screenwriting, nor did they use their income from screenwriting to support other writing endeavors. They dedicated their creative energies towards writing for television and motion pictures.

Minority writers drew upon a wide range of resources when developing ideas. Approximately half the writers referred to outside sources, including books, short stories, magazine and newspaper articles. One Latino writer outlined her approach:

I get my ideas from TV and film and magazines and articles and talking to friends and things I make up or things I can imagine and things like that. That's it...sometimes the best ideas actually come from things that happened to people that I know...for instance, one of the scripts I wrote received a lot of mail. It was a very, very nice script, very beautiful, very sensitive, funny, but very, very sad...it had to do with a young girl who sees her father at a restaurant with another woman and here she is confronted with her father's infidelity and how it hurts her even more than if she had seen her husband or boyfriend or whatever with another woman. Well, a friend of mine had an experience that she told me about when she was little, she saw her uncle with another woman. Well, somehow or other, I kind of thought about it in my head and I decided to kind of form this whole thing around this character and her father...this was nominated for an Emmy by the way.

In general, old movies served as the most frequent points of departure for script development. "I get a lot of ideas from old movies," one writer explained. "If you see a lot of Lucas and Spielberg stuff...it's from old movies. I am working on a screenplay that is an updated version of *Lilies of the Field,* so it's derivative in a way from that and also from Spencer Tracy and Bing Crosby, *Going My Way* and *Boys' Town.* So you know you take those basically good dramatic pieces and structures...and you see how...you change them in a way that it's going to be faster and it's going to be still dramatic and still funny." Similarly, an African-American writer reported working on a screenplay derived from the film *Picnic.* By relocating the story in a trailer park instead of a small town, he was able to create new dramatic developments.

Despite their minority identification, these writers often referred to movies and televisions shows that featured white or Anglo casts and production staffs. Minority writers explained their use of "white" television and films as a decision based on creative quality, not ethnic content. "I write well-rounded, solid material," one Latino writer explained. "My tutors, my mentors, are people that do films like *Wuthering Heights, Grapes of Wrath, How Green Was My Valley.* I like slices of life that have meat to them."

Additional motives may underlie these choices. First, minority writers may unconsciously identify with the white majority, despite protests to the contrary. Second, minority writers may simply be making astute "business" decisions, building ideas from works with records of critical and financial success. Third, there are few successful minority-oriented projects for writers to draw upon, although this reality is now changing. Using such limited material may diminish their own marketability and future success. However, such ideas are pure speculation, few minority writers discussed their reasons for selecting "white" films as creative resources.

"It's been fun," one writer claimed. "I have really, for the first time, been able to get paid for something and had fun doing it because I was able to go through and not use my own ideas and hide behind somebody else. Not that I ripped people off but I would take things I saw in the *Lucy Show*, and *Laurel and Hardy*, and combine them and mix them up and all that and then when the producers said, 'No,' I didn't sit there and take it personally and get pissed." There was less personal risk in going to "objective" and impersonal sources rather than submitting private experience to external judgment. However, minority writers using "outside" sources did not appear involved with their work to the same degree as writers who worked from personal experience.

One-half of the minority writers depended primarily on personal experience as a creative resource. "So far, my ideas have come from my own life and own experience," one writer remarked. "I believe most writers take from their own experience." Another writer offered a detailed account of her creative practices:

Where do my ideas come from? I just sit down with a blank piece of paper and you think you're not going to come up with anything and then the page just starts filling up—an idea can feed on another idea and you'll go back and cross them out and say, "I did that." But you just have to sit down and it has to be quiet for me, I can't be around a lot of other people. Writing can be kind of painful for me, in a way, because it's like pulling things out of yourself and that's what I mean about it being a part of you—you're looking towards your own experience, you are giving a part of yourself to a script, to an idea and once you're done, you feel real good about it. But at the time, it just hurts.

Hers was not an exclusively female reaction. A male African-American writer explained that "When I am working as a writer, I put myself in a frame of mind where creativity is possible...I might have to sit alone for days or weeks and hope that some idea would trigger off in my brain. The last screenplay that I wrote came about because of something very personal that was so compelling I felt I had to write it. It was basically about my early life in the South and my family's life and things that we had to confront just to get out of that kind of sharecropper situation."

Minority writers who drew upon their private experience for script development offered lengthy explanations of how ideas evolved, confirming a profound investment in their work. One disabled Latino writer recalled:

The second screenplay I wrote was called *De Los Muertos*, which means "of" or "from the dead." It's about a guy who comes back from Nam. I wrote this in '73 when the war was just ending up. He comes back, he had been MIA for eight years, he had left his family and when he came back he wanted to put the eight years back, he didn't want to catch up...and he had trouble adjusting. I really used that as a metaphor for my blindness, because at that time I hadn't seen anything in about ten years, so that everything I had seen was ten years old...so I kind of used that as a metaphor where the guy from Nam comes back and has not seen anything for ten years, so I said, "What would happen if I gained my sight back, what kind of world would it be?" I would be like a prisoner coming back who hadn't seen it and he'd be looking for everything that was there and even though he could see it, he wouldn't accept it. So I really worked hard on that script.

This was a particularly emotional accounting, although the writer added that the script never sold because of its Vietnam theme in an anti-war era.

Several minority writers observed that the quality of their writing improved once they began to draw upon emotional and personal experience. "I get my ideas a lot from emotions that I feel," one writer recalled. "I used to have a real intellectual approach...I'm saying that negatively. I would start out with some kind of concept of some kind of frame in which to write, some interesting way to frame something, for example, the way *Betrayal* was structured. I would try to think of something that was neat and then I would figure out a story to put into it so usually I would have these clever gimmicks that were very empty." Like their majority counterparts, minority writers communicated intimate concerns through their screenplays. "I wrote another script... really because I was going through a lot personally," a writer commented, "a lot of friends of mine were getting married...and it seemed to be like an epidemic and I wondered what was causing it. Why people who had been comfortably living together...decided to get married and...also I was going through a romance in my life and I brought that into the script. And so the script had a lot to do with the nature of love and sacrifice and commitment and what it means...although it's still not quite there, that's the script that so far has come most from my heart."

Similar to this account, other minority writers reported using their writing as a way of "working through" rather ordinary personal problems. "You look towards your own experiences sometimes," one woman explained, "and sometimes you think, 'What would I like to see a character like this do?' Maybe it's even similar to an experience you've had or a problem you have and you think, 'What would happen if I did it the other way?'"

"Writing became very important to me," a disabled Latino writer explained, "it became the way I saw my past and kept the visual part of my life alive, all through my dreams and through my writing."

The personal nature of these writers' remarks resembled those of majority individuals. However, they differed significantly. Majority writers discussed how they translated personal dilemmas into film or television scripts. Their own experience was somehow "broadened" for audience appeal. Few minority writers described casting their personal histories in such broadened terms. Instead, their visions often remained personal.

While both used personal experience, minority writers drew more specifically on their own cultural backgrounds. "I always knew and you always hear, writing is a very personal thing, it's about as personal as you can get," one writer explained, "and I kept thinking, I gotta write as a person of color..." His preoccupation with his cultural background was echoed by a Latino male who commented, "Although I am not a strong Catholic, a lot of my themes have to do with faith and sacrifice and even to the point of borrowing from the *Bible* or mythology of whatever and turning it on its head...I wrote a script called *The Virgin* about what if that were to happen today?" Personal experience served as a useful, if unreliable, form of writing capital to be drawn upon, with varying degrees of success. What remained unclear was whether the minority character of these writers' experience had to be "bleached" or creatively neutralized in order to succeed. Why did certain minority writers succeed writing scripts from private experiences while other writers failed?

Successful minority writers combined personal experience with outside resources including short stories, books, news stories, and magazine articles. "My scripts have been about feelings I've had," one writer began. "One started as an intellectual notion but it was also based on an article I saw in the newspaper...it was based on an actual incident and then I just went off from there. I said, 'Why would this happen? What does it mean?' And then from the theme, I worked out the story."

Additionally, successful minority writers applied personal experience in such a way that they transcended minority-majority differences. These individuals attempted to reconcile their identities as minorities and people of color with their identities as artists. One writer explained:

Well, I like to write about the human condition but certainly being black has put a different flavor on reality that I think should certainly be there if you're going to try to capture that experience...Race has certainly become a factor in some of my writing and it should become a factor in anybody's writing. If you're white you have a certain experience and if you're black you have a certain experience. And I also think that there are a lot of shades within the race that you can tell about too, in stories. Blacks look just as differently as whites do and there are many stories within the African-American community to write about and I try not to say, "Well, blacks are this and blacks are that." I try to write about individual blacks and give them the full human dimension and flesh their characters out so that we see them as total human beings. I don't write about blacks in general. I try to pick a family or individual who is black and allow that to reflect this is a black in this situation and show how the individual functions within it.

These writers did not so much surrender their minority identities as recast them in a more universal form. Screenplays were not based literally on life events. Instead, incidents were disguised and reworked until the script assumed its final creative form. A Latino writer summarized this process:

> There was a script I wrote very much influenced by Sam Shepard's work but really very, very personal, ultimately—although I based it on another character. I based the main character on somebody I knew, it wasn't based on myself but there was a relationship with his parents [in the script] and the parents were based on my parents and what I saw that had happened to them was mostly about stagnation and how one tragedy can cause things to stagnate; even though there was no one tragedy in my parents' lives...they were both alcoholics and it was just a constant repetitious situation where they would argue, there was a sick dependence that was keeping them together and so that's basically what the script was about—how, if you don't move on, you don't see the possibility of changes. It's not going to be there. And how you get involved in relationships that you need but are harmful to you at the same time and so anything you write is bound to be personal, it can't be totally removed.

Similarly, other minority writers discussed character development at length, identifying with the individuals they created and the situations they encountered. "You kind of immerse yourself in one character and then you go into the other character, and you keep going back and forth," one veteran black writer stated. "You pretty much know what they're going to say, how they're going to say it, and sometimes it all comes out."

One female writer related problems involving a main character based on an actual individual. "The real woman was quite a package," the writer recalled, "she was not what you exactly call admirable. I first saw her walking down the hall in the hospital, barefoot, dressed from head to toe in black leather, with flaming red hair. She was screaming, using every foul word you can imagine—I really had to clean her up for the screenplay. In real life she was a big drug user and probably even a dealer. There were contracts on her life—and at one point I thought she had been killed." The writer struggled to preserve the character's strength and uniqueness while making her acceptable to movie audiences. In the process, the writer's involvement with the character grew into an obsession; she experienced the completion of the script as "an exorcism and a loss."

For other minority writers, characters embodied ideal traits and counteracted stereotypes. The creation of believable characters was a source of tremendous pride for these writers, validating their minority identities and representing an important creative accomplishment.

Control

Discussions of the creative process invariably turned to the issue of control. Once established in Hollywood, many encountered difficulties as screenwriters that equaled or even exceeded their problems as minorities. The emphasis on creative control increased relative to the success of the writer interviewed. With noted minority writers, familiar complaints surfaced. "When you sell your screenplay, you're out of it, baby," one successful writer snapped. "You have nothing else to say about your screenplay for the life of your screenplay. You might not even recognize it when it comes to the screen and there is nothing you can do about it."

"There is so much garbage involved," another minority writer complained. "It's not a question of being an artist and writing something and having it produced because you know, no matter what you write, 50 million people are going to change it and broadcast standards are going to come in and you have not got one bit of control over what you write."

Minority like majority writers complained bitterly that producers who lacked creative skills ordered arbitrary script changes simply to exert authority. "I've seen good writers who really got their work screwed by people who may not really know what they're doing, who don't really understand the writing process, who come in and tell you what to do," one black female writer recalled, "and it's a way of justifying their jobs too. They can't just sit back and say nothing, because then what are they there for?"

Another writer recalled an incident involving a politically oriented script she had written concerning two Texas ranching families and their struggle for emotional and economic survival. At the direction of a producer whose past experience encompassed crime shows, the writer rewrote the script as a criminally oriented story involving mafia manipulation of meat prices, elaborating that:

I was put in a position of developing a mafia story and having to deal with, first of all, an incredible amount of illogic to make that work. And I remember it being 3:00 in the morning and I am sitting in the office, on the lot, trying to figure out how...I came up with it and I did it, but in the course of all these changes, they [the production staff] got less and less satisfied because what they were after was to my mind foreign. And finally I got a letter back from the producer after the show had been cancelled—the script was never even shot—and I got a letter back from him that said something to the effect that "I couldn't even bear to see the script tortured into something it didn't seem to want to be, which was exactly what had happened..."

This writer's experience was not unusual. Another writer detailed how an entire script he wrote was transformed, including mundane changes in characters' names as well as extensive revisions of dialogue, characterizations, and ending. While saying he was "appalled" and "heartsick," this writer also admitted that "this was my first inkling of what goes on in this industry and continues to go on today. It has nothing to do with being a person of color or gay or a woman but it has to do with simply being a writer and the status of writers in the entertainment industry."

It is a central reality in Hollywood that all writers lack control. However, for minority individuals, their sense of powerlessness was often exacerbated by ethnic, sexual, and racial discord between writers, directors, and production staffs. Decisions majority writers characterized as "business," were interpreted by minority writers as racist, sexist, or related to whatever bias in minority-majority relationships they specified.

Minority writers recounted several incidents involving cross-cultural conflict. One writer recounted the struggle for control of a television project he originally created with two other African-American writers. The proposed series was designed to offer an authentic yet entertaining portrait of African-American family life along with providing opportunities for black writers and producers. Unfortunately, he recalled, "the network said that if the project was going to go forward they wanted the executive producer to do the rest of the writing on the show and they wanted the script totally rewritten. They said that they had big problems with the script...we had to give that up. We had to allow the executive producer, then with his partner, to write the show...and they were white." The producer prevailed and the black writers were dismissed.

Minority writers claimed that "stars" also interfered with script content. "The actor becomes very jealous of...how his character is used," one Latino writer explained, "so sometimes he will say to the writers, 'I will not do that, I will not say that,' and we've got to satisfy him too!"

Criticism was directed at both minority and majority actors. In the most awkward situations, writers found themselves caught between minority stars and majority producers or directors in fights for control. One writer recalled such a dilemma:

The executive producer was white, we had a producer who was black, the other team of producers was white, the other team of writers was white and then we got another writing team that was black. It was wonderful. The only person who made any trouble was the star. The most difficult problems occurred between what the writers of the show wanted to do with the show and what the star wanted to do with it. We all realized something later—that the star was living her life through the show, the way she would have liked to live her life...She brought up her kids alone and it was always a struggle for her and after we wanted to write a part-time job for her character, she absolutely refused...And she was so unrealistic about the relationship between a man and a woman. She wanted these lines in: "You're the head of the household and I should have shown you the proper respect," and even the men on the staff said, "...these are really not things you should be sending out to the public." So it was very difficult...but she's the one who's bringing in the viewers. Nobody knows my name, nobody knows the executive producer, nobody knows anybody that works in the network—but they sure know her name.

Ironically, in this particular account, while the writer and star were both women of color, the writer ultimately identified with the racially mixed production staff.

As they described struggling for a voice, minority writers recalled their extreme and emotional reactions. "How did I feel?" one writer asked. "I fought with them and I fought with them and I said, how would they dare to ask me to change a script that I believed in so completely...then I had to come up with a compromise, and I did."

Anger followed by resignation figured in other writers' responses. "You have to sit there and shut up and your insides are being torn apart," one woman writer remarked, "but there is nothing you can do about it."

Revisions provoked particular distress. "It hurts," one female writer commented, "especially when you know it's wrong. If I could look at it and say, 'Okay, they made it better,' I'd understand but there were a lot of times when the rewrites are done and they are done by more experienced people and I could see where they made it better—but when it's done and it makes it worse, it hurts."

Several writers complained when their scripts were revised by other writers, claiming control—not script content—was at issue. One writer described a battle of wills:

Larry Gelbart is a writer, he's a compulsive writer, he just rewrites everything...the man thinks he is perfect—he just has to do that. So you know that you better not hand your script in until 20 minutes before you go on the air so he won't change it...but I did a thing for a production company and I was invited out to dinner and while I was gone he rewrote the whole goddamned script and didn't write it better, just rewrote it arbitrarily. When you have someone saying "Hello" he rewrites it as "Hi." The funny thing is—he didn't want any credit, he just couldn't stand to leave it alone...he can't. He did it all the time on *MASH*. He's got to have control.

When asked how he responded to such revisions, another writer explained that, "You develop a tough hide, It's painful, awful, you sit there—I think it's happened to almost everything that I've written, especially for television—but it's still difficult. How much control do we have over the words we write? That anyone else can come in and change it around any way that they want to and sometimes it's not the directors, it's not the producers—even the actors change it. That's what's great about someone like Spike Lee—these things never happen to him."

In dealing with their lack of decision-making authority, minority writers developed several adaptive strategies. While some writers rationalized script changes as being a strategic necessity, others claimed that revisions were creatively valid. One Latino woman recalled making alterations in a screenplay and ultimately agreeing with the suggestions of the white producers in charge.

Strategies used by minority writers depended on their positions as well as what was at stake. Many individuals combined immediate compromise with delayed gratification, a tactic practiced by their majority colleagues. These screenwriters resolved control issues by "giving in" to current demands and promising themselves future control. The African-American writer who helped create the television series that was later assigned to a white production staff exhibited such an approach:

We had to give up too much on that idea so that when it got on the screen it was perhaps 50% of what we had originally envisioned...the way I look at that [is that]...in order to establish some credibility, you're going to have to give up a lot on this first, we're going to have to give up a lot to get the project done but at least they'll see some of what we're talking about and then the key is that for the next deal on the next project, you give up less, we compromise less, so that each time you get a little more control until you finally get the opportunity to do the thing the way you see it...those are the steps that you have to take and you have to know that you have to be patient, that it's going to take a little bit of time and that you'll eventually get there. That's the reality of the business.

Other minority writers revealed extensive plans for expanding their roles in the entertainment industry, branching into directing and producing. One writer succinctly explained he intended "to direct because that is the ultimate in terms of controlling your own writing. If you write a screenplay—and writers will tell you about this all the time—you write a screenplay and even if the screenplay is not changed all that much, the director is going to take full credit for the picture, including the screenplay. Look at *Boyz N the Hood*—Singleton did everything and got credit for everything. But then you look at *American Me*, no one knows the writer but everyone knows the star-slash-director—Edward James Olmos."

Most minority writers wished to expand their creative roles in the future and exert more control over projects. However a small group of writers conveyed a sense of resignation and spoke of leaving the industry. One writer candidly admitted, "I don't know. How long do I want to play the game, much longer? How much do I want to give. Can I slide through?" Another writer despaired, "I am forty years old and I don't want to fight every fight anymore...I am limited to what I can do."

One black writer candidly discussed her lack of future plans. Her indecision typified the uncertainty confronting all writers in Hollywood, irrespective of status: "I don't know what I would like to end up doing. Where I want to be in ten years. I don't know where I am going to be five years from now, I really don't. I barely know year to year—it's a strange, strange business. There is absolutely no security here and you can be gone tomorrow, but for the worst reasons in the world."

In the end, these individuals indicated their desire to continue working in the industry. Several writers expressed the need to portray their personal experience and contribute something meaningful to audiences and artistry, integrating specific minority interests with more global human concerns. One successful male African-American writer-producer spoke eloquently:

> I want this work to reflect who I am...I hope that it will reflect something about myself and how I feel about life. I know it's a cliché but I would certainly like to leave something behind for my kids and for the people who have given me so much, having believed in me. I'd like to leave something of value that reflects my gratitude to those people for keeping me alive and surviving...I would like to let them know that it was worth it. I hope that I can do something that they can say, "Well, he was worth it and he did something good."

His concern was universal, reaching across boundaries of ethnicity and sex, even across the geography of Hollywood.

Notes

[1]While all shared certain concerns, no prototypical minority writer emerged. Unlike their white male counterparts, these individuals did not exhibit one typical minority experience. Instead, their approach to their work, to Hollywood, and to one another differed remarkably between groups. In later sections, these differences will be explored. However, initially minority writers will be described as one set—examining similarities where they occur—in background, response to Hollywood, identity, creativity, and control.

[2]Only two writers, both Latino, totally rejected identification with any minority and denied encountering any type of discrimination in Hollywood. Still, each had taken advantage of opportunities available to minorities—programs designed to correct past inequities. "I felt that I was helped along by my last name," one admitted. "I would think if they asked you—I was a minority." The other writer stated that he had obtained his first staff writing position by qualifying as the requisite minority writer for a studio. Although both writers used their minority status to their advantage when opportunities arose, they denied its importance otherwise.

[3]McClintick (1982) has described Yiddish as the "unofficial language of Hollywood."

Chapter Six

✦ ✦ ✦

No One Knows Our Names

Minority writers' experience in Hollywood was marked by a mixture of ambition, mistrust, gratitude, and hostility, combining to create a profound sense of separation. Ultimately, their discomfort focused on the issue of discrimination. Writers claimed they were denied professional opportunities for reasons having nothing to do with talent or ability. Judgments were rendered and rejections were made, they felt, due to sex, age, ethnicity and race. With two exceptions[1] every writer reported experiencing discrimination, even those individuals who had achieved success and acceptance in Hollywood. While majority writers objected to being discriminated against simply as writers, minorities felt discriminated against as writers *and* as members of underrepresented groups. This duality left them no room to develop identities as an elite.

According to the writers interviewed, discrimination pervaded the entertainment industry, affecting minority writers at every turn. They could not "break into" the industry and were frustrated in their efforts to secure and maintain positions in studios or with networks. In addition, writers faced difficulty selling material. Most painful, however, was the overall unwillingness of the white establishment to accept them as professional equals and colleagues. Minority writers felt their presence went unacknowledged, that they did not truly belong to the Hollywood elite. "We are in the Guild," one writer stated, "but nobody knows our names."

Minorities felt that they received somewhat less than equal the opportunities of their white male counterparts. In assessing their careers, minority writers compared their own accomplishments to what occurred around them with a sense of disquiet. One writer could not avoid making comparisons while outlining his professional background:

On one hand, people constantly say to me, "Gee, you've done well, and you've moved quite far in a relatively short period of time," but I tend not to look at it that way because I know that at the time I came into this business, there were other people who came in with about the same qualifications as myself, who are not of the same color that I am, whose careers progressed much more rapidly and I've always felt that I had at least as much to offer and I don't think it's any secret in Hollywood that it's much tougher for minorities to get ahead in this business. It's a very tough business, very competitive for anybody, but particularly for ethnic minorities who are just not there, who are just not represented.

His reaction was not unusual. There was a constant refrain from minority individuals, each of whom believed things would have been altogether different "…if I were white and male." These writers shared the identical perception that given that one change, with everything else remaining the same, they would have achieved considerably greater financial and creative success. Additionally, writers believed their frustration was an understandable and legitimate response to the discrimination they experienced. This preoccupation with discrimination distinguished minority writers from their majority counterparts and united them as a group. For minority writers, discrimination was the tie that binds.

Forms of Discrimination

Discrimination made its presence known in varying forms—some emotionally discomforting and others affecting minority progress and power in Hollywood. Initially, several minority writers reported hearing remarks with racist or anti-minority overtones. Such remarks were reportedly commonplace in the entertainment industry. One writer recalled:

We wrote a script and we started taking it around and we were so, so, so badly received, in spite of the fact that our workshop leader was being congratulated by these same people on how well he was teaching us. The same people that were congratulating him and patting him on the back, they were not opening doors for us and were saying just the most degrading remarks, for instance, "Oh, when the Mexicans get out of East L.A., then they don't know where they are" and things like, "Well, the reason that there aren't any Hispanic writers is that they just don't have it in them, Hispanics can't write."

Another writer recounted how one producer constantly referred to gays in the industry as "faggots." While his remarks did not involve her directly, she found them offensive nonetheless. A Latino writer recalled a white executive producer asking him if he carried a switchblade. In other instances, many minorities described how white writers and producers, forgetting they were present, uttered racial slurs. One African-American writer related how a group of Anglo writers and producers, casting a film, discussed their need for a "big nigger," ignoring her presence. They later apologized, explaining, "you know we were joking."

These remarks, while inflammatory, were not the key concern of minority writers. Most writers, while expressing indignation at these statements, were resigned to their existence. More serious protests were reserved for problems and discriminatory practices that writers felt directly affected their chances to succeed in the industry.

First, many individuals felt that they could not obtain information that would help them in Hollywood. One writer, using a sports metaphor, explained:

The most important thing is we don't know what those rules are and as soon as we learn them they change: "I am sorry today we are not using the football, we are using the baseball." "I am sorry, tomorrow we are using the tennis racket, we are not using the baseball anymore." And that's what's sad. The in-group doesn't tell you what the rules are. If you hear right now they are going to be doing *Home Alone* movies, it's too late. By the time I sit down and if I write my *Home Alone* script, they'll say, "I'm sorry, everybody had a *Home Alone* script on the board, they're bought and being done...we're doing something else. We're doing *Little Red Riding Hood*. By the time you hear it...see that's where the in-group comes in. They all know each other, the agents know them, they have lunches. How is it that if you look at a TV guide all the action shows that week or within a two-week period all do the same kind of show? They have lunch together, they talk about the same thing. I get my ideas maybe by talking to you, by talking to somebody else. They get their ideas over at The Ivy during their low-cholesterol lunch. They all run home and they write the same thing, because they got the same stimulation at the same time.

This feeling of not knowing the "rules" stemmed from minorities' dislocation from the Hollywood establishment. Minority writers contended they remained "in the dark" concerning current trends in the industry, unaware what types of projects were being sought by studios and networks. This lack of information affected their ability to pitch projects or sell scripts as one writer explained:

You're not there being motivated by all the things that are going on in a company...even when I've talked to, for instance, secretaries that work for Universal, they know things, they know more than I do and if they have higher ambitions, it helps that they are being bombarded with information constantly, "So and so is doing this..." "No, we don't like this because of this and that." And "this and this works better than this and that." They are there constantly learning, accumulating all that information, and they're going to be able to sell a script! When you're on the outside, the only sources that you have are the same sources that everybody else has and because I don't have access to any inside information, how will I know what sells?

Another writer recalled a situation where he lacked inside information. "At the time that we [the writer and his partner] worked on *Empty Nest* they were doing a lot of issue-oriented shows. We submitted the script and were told, 'We're no longer doing issue-oriented shows,' and by the time they officially rejected it they were doing them again so, unless you have those inside sources, you really are taking a total gamble."

Along with difficulties acquiring industry information, minorities described a second form of discrimination: the unfair scrutiny they claimed their writing received. Many stated that they were held to more exacting standards and afforded less flexibility than white writers. Minorities reported that they were expected to be "super" writers. "A minority writer does a script and the script, as all scripts, needs work," one writer explained. "They are tougher on that than they are on a white writer's script. They say, 'Ah, it didn't work but you know, we gave the guy a chance,' and I say, 'Wait a minute! You give one black writer a chance and you give a hundred white writers a chance and we know what the problems are when you deal with writers—why?'"

Several writers claimed the rationale behind such scrutiny was not the protection of quality entertainment. Instead, the concept of creative "standards" provided Hollywood powers with an easy out: minorities could be rejected on the basis of their work. This allowed the powerful to evade accusations of discrimination. Instead, producers simply stated that minority writing was inadequate and not up to the appropriate standards. Just what these standards were, no one was certain. One writer offered a hypothetical example:

So, okay, let's talk about what Stephen Bochco might do—he has a lot of shows on...he can't write them all. So what he does is, he's got to hire people to do that. So you go to Bochco and say, "Steve, why don't you hire some black writers?" [imitating answer] "I think I am going to, it's a good idea," and he never does. "Good idea, yeah, right, send me somebody." And then you send them somebody and they say, "She didn't quite make it. His or her work wasn't quite up to par..." Yeah, right, right.

It is unclear whether minorities, in fact, are subjected to standards that differ from those applied to majority writers. Still, minorities insisted differing standards existed and were part of the discrimination they experienced in Hollywood.

A third problem stemming from discrimination concerned the lack of professional advancement among minorities. Individuals observed that there were few minority story editors, writer-producers, or writer-directors; that overall not many minorities held positions with any actual decision-making power or influence. White male writers enjoyed professional advancement as well as enhanced opportunities within the Hollywood structure, while minorities were bypassed and all but ignored. One writer observed:

You really feel like there is no future really in it. I've seen so many bright guys at the network—black guys—they let them go so far: Peter Andrews, Roy Campanella, and then they say, "Fine, okay, we made you vice-president of creative affairs," which is a bullshit title, then there's nothing else but then they promote everyone else above them so then they finally leave. But what happens is when the white guys leave they get a berth at the studio immediately and they have built these favors up so they immediately make the money they didn't make when they were at the network. This doesn't go on when black guys leave. They either get some token thing, while everyone else goes out of their way to have deals already set and laid in. You'd like to say that there were other reasons for it and all, but what it boils down to absolutely has to be racism, there's no question, because you look at the level of your work and the level of your credits and you look at the level of other people's credits and somebody is going to have to come through that.

The complaints registered in this account were echoed by several other minority writers. Obviously it was not merely access to the industry that minorities felt they were denied. Even if they achieved success at lower-level positions, minorities carried little hope of advancing to positions of far-reaching power. "I was rewarded with salary and promotions to a point," one writer bitterly stated, "and at a certain point they'd say, 'Get to the back of the bus,' and I said, 'Fuck you.'"

Out of his rage, this writer quit a lucrative staff position. Still, despite these protests, minority frustration went largely unnoticed. Minority writers felt they expendable, once their creativity and experience were exploited, they were thrown aside by the Hollywood establishment. An African-American writer outlining one production company's practice explained, "They got the brain-storm: 'We'll have an apprentice program, we can pay them anything, they'll have a term contract, there's no guarantee and if we get somebody that we like, then we can start them off at the bottom.' So that's what they did. As soon as someone got to that point, they'd fire him and hire someone else, and by that time they had learned enough about black idiom and black parlance and slang and culture to write it themselves."

Once Anglo writers had proven they could follow up and write ethnic minority characters, minority writers were dismissed from projects and denied any lasting access or control. One television project with an African-American theme developed by black writers was sold, scheduled for network broadcast, and was reassigned to white writers.

Writers objected to being exploited for something more basic than their experience as minorities: their status. Many claimed token hiring occurred on the infrequent occasions when Hollywood powers addressed minority dissatisfaction. One minority writer would be contracted for a writing staff or one minority script would be bought by a studio, but no substantial change occurred. Instead, these were holding efforts as the Hollywood establishment attempted to placate minority demands for equal access and opportunity. Writers criticized the individuals they felt allowed themselves to be used—supposedly free agents representing minority interests—but really powerless tokens allaying majority guilt. One black writer openly ridiculed another writer turned executive:

It's so blatantly racist. They're simply just setting up someone so they can point to them and say they're willing to pay them. You look at Stan Robertson at

Columbia a few years ago. Stan has never done a picture. He's never done anything. He was a newspaper reporter and Columbia simply hired him as a public relations guy. Yet when you would have a meeting with him he would tell you, "Now if we're willing to work up some kind of deal...anything you write has to go through me. You can't go elsewhere." Why in the hell should I bring you everything? You're not giving me any deal on it. You're not putting this into development. You couldn't if you wanted to. Have you seen his name on anything? I mean he took a lot of meetings, that's what he was paid to do, just sit there and be a buffer. Columbia was not about to—because of their product image—about to alienate any ethnic groups so they simply had somebody who's going to meet them and he had a girl who's Latino who was his assistant, so that looked good...but he had no power.

In addition to charges of tokenism, minorities insisted the industry establishment did not actively recruit or employ writers from under-represented groups. The powerful in Hollywood hired those writers who shared their own backgrounds—white Jewish males under 40—while paying lip service to the idea of hiring ethnic minority individuals. Excusing their responsibility for the absence of minority talent, Hollywood powers were quoted as asking, "Where are the minority writers? We would hire them if we could find them!" Their questions were artificial, minority writers insisted, and the Hollywood establishment was accused of simply not caring. "Producers say, 'We're not racist, we don't go out attacking black people,'" one writer claimed. "But I say, 'You don't care, you just watch things around you turn to nothing while you do nothing. You aren't doing anything and the things that you do whenever you have an opportunity to hire a minority person, you do not.'"

Stereotypes
Minority writers maintained discrimination in Hollywood involved more than biased hiring practices. They charged that Hollywood's portrayal of underrepresented groups consisted largely of stereotypes, with little regard for variation within specific minority groups. Arguing that Hollywood's depiction of minorities had strongly influenced audiences, writers were concerned with the images the industry communicated. According to these writers, expectations of minorities were shaped by what their counterparts did in television and film. All too often, on-screen images translated to off-screen reality.

Several writers critiqued scripts that depicted minorities and their lives as a cliché, pointing to the discrimination inherent in such projects. One physically challenged writer discussed the stereotyping fostered by "crip scripts," with story lines featuring a disabled person being emotionally fortified through an encounter with a "normal" person who urges them to accept their disability and move ahead in the world. Similarly, numerous African-American writers objected to what they labeled "nigger" shows. Chief among the offenders was CBS's and Linda-Bloodworth-Thomason's highly successful series, *Evening Shade*, which one black female writer maintained was drawn from the ideas "Southern whites and Liberal Jews" held about African-Americans. "Do you see Ossie Davis on that show?" she asked, "He's as bad as Steppin' Fetchit. And the whites think they're cool because they eat at his rib joint." Another black writer half-jokingly asked, "I mean, blacks *have* been on television but when you look at *Homefront*, I mean, whose family is that? I didn't know anybody's black family being helped by whites after World War II. I didn't know anybody who was helped by whites, no one!!"

Several writers assessed Hollywood's characterization of black males as weak, dependent, or altogether absent. "I always felt that the black male is invisible on American television as a strong character," a black writer remarked, "but I wanted to see on television, or in the movies, a dominant black man who cared, who was responsible, who wasn't just jive talking, who didn't say, 'in yo' face' and 'up side yo' head' and all that stuff and who was not upscale educated, a guy with a normal education, not a guy who makes it down to Wall Street every morning. A guy who's a working stiff like most people are and who had beliefs and who had some kind of morality and some kind of dignity." Similarly, a Latino writer focused on the stereotypical portrayal of her minority group, insisting that Latinos are inevitably depicted as, "illegal aliens, drug abusers, prostitutes and of course, housekeepers."

In discussing how stereotypes could be altered and how minorities should be portrayed, the idea of "balance" was recurrently invoked. For balance to be achieved, writers argued, minorities should be cast neither as deviants nor ideals. "If I was going to use women or Asians or Latinos in comedies, I want to see them in dramatic roles as well," one writer argued. "If I portrayed one of them as the bad guy, I wanted to see one as a responsible human being. Not that I wanted to whitewash, excuse the expression, all minorities, but I wanted people to say that, 'they're just like we are.'"

Several individuals worked to change how minorities were portrayed, detailing their efforts at altering script content riddled with stereotypes. One individual recalled a confrontation involving stereotypes that occurred 15 years earlier:

I was really upset. There was a skit on *Tony Orlando and Dawn* with the two black singers...when they started out they were two black girls living together kind of in the ghetto and they had a nice little apartment where you saw the kitchen usually and over the weeks, over the episodes, the set decorator changed it...The refrigerator got dirtier and dirtier. It's like with brown stains all over it and there was one of those stereotypical black velvet pictures or a poster, I forget which, but it was stuck on the wall. They made the refrigerator dirty instead of clean, they made it dingy looking, yellowed it up and I noticed that and I mentioned it finally. It was bothering me but then they started using stereotypes in the episodes, things in the little skits, stealing, drinking, welfare, and all those sorts of things so I mentioned that to a producer...I just mentioned it. I didn't want to, and it bothered me to have to mention it, but I did.

This writer's reluctance to confront the producer was not atypical. Many minority writers experienced a conflict between personal security and group concerns, struggling with the dilemma of how to remain true to their minority identity and advance professionally in Hollywood. They could not concentrate on their success in Hollywood and ignore the content of what was produced by the industry in which they struggled to belong.

Most minority writers outlined future writing projects aimed at revising Hollywood's portrayal of minorities, insisting that their work as writers serve a purpose beyond personal fulfillment. However, they felt restricted in what they could accomplish.

Limited Expertise

According to minority writers, their creative abilities served as an object of discrimination. They accused the Hollywood establishment of believing minority writers were only capable of writing scripts about the groups to which they belonged. When asked why his writing had not sold, one writer offered what was soon to become a familiar explanation, that minorities were limited to writing about their own groups. "Black writers can only write about black themes is one story you'll hear constantly," he explained. "White writers can write about blacks. White writers can write about disability and white male writers can write about women. Women, black writers, and disabled writers can't write about anything except their own universe, which is one of the great lies you run into in this business."

This perception of what is best termed "limited expertise" emerged as a consistent theme in minority discussions of industry discrimination. Numerous examples supported their contention that the Hollywood establishment perceived minority creativity as limited. In describing their experiences, minority writers with varied backgrounds all shared the feeling that they were pigeonholed by the white establishment of Hollywood. A physically challenged writer explained:

I called a producer and said, "I would like to come in and pitch a story to you," and his response was, "Well...we've got *Life Goes On* this season, call me next year," and I was not going to pitch a disabled story to him but I was so shocked by his reaction that I just never bothered to call him again, at least in terms of pitching anything. That's an attitude you run into. Being a physically challenged writer, it's assumed that's what I want to write about, that's what I *can* write about.

This was not an uncommon experience. An African-American writer encountered a narrowing of expectations and opportunities once he ended his professional association with a white male collaborator. "I went into comedy writing and I didn't realize it," he remarked, "all of a sudden I was writing only black shows and because of thinking as long as there were good performers, I didn't care who I was writing for and it didn't really dawn on me until then..." Minority writers were extremely wary of being restricted to working only on minority projects. They were able to write across ethnic and racial lines, claiming that in order to assimilate they were forced to explore and understand majority culture, growing up as "experts" on mainstream America. An African-American writer offered:

I don't know how a white man can write about black experience but I certainly should be able to write about white experiences, having lived in white houses. I have an insight. And having lived with white people, and been part of white institutions all my life, I understand that part very well. But then at home, it's my own black experience so I would feel...that I would be very qualified to write the white experience and the black then vice versa, 'cause I don't know of any white people who have ever lived in a black household, but most black people have lived within the white establishment, if they've ever gone to a school, if they've ever gone to a bank or had a job, they've been part of the white establishment. Very few white people work for a black company. Very few white people have worked for black families in a service capacity...So for those kinds of reasons, it seems to me, that if I can write, that I would be better equipped to handle both situations.

A few writers had worked on "white" projects. But the individuals who had been able to write for such productions were labeled exceptions or, worse still, tokens "allowed" to work on such projects because of equal opportunity requirements within the industry. Establishment-sponsored projects available to minorities were ultimately viewed as superficial, as motivated by the wrong impulse or as simply not enough—a case of too little too late.

This was not always the case. Certain minority-majority relationships succeeded despite the surrounding atmosphere of competition and mistrust. A few successful minority writers described help they had received from their supposed nemesis: the white establishment of Hollywood. These writers acknowledged the individuals who had served as mentors, offering a combination of emotional encouragement and practical support. Mentors reviewed writing, introduced professional contacts, and made job referrals. Minorities who developed associations with mentors gave these individuals significant credit for their subsequent success in Hollywood. "Well, one thing that you have to have," a black female writer explained, "is a mentor. You have to have someone out there helping you, there is absolutely no way that you can do it alone."

In acknowledging their mentors, several writers mentioned names recognized both in and outside of Hollywood. One individual recounted how he broke into the entertainment industry through the efforts of the late Steve McQueen. Another writer recalled that while working as an actor he met author Harold Robbins, who encouraged him to write and subsequently helped him establish contacts in television and films. Similarly, an African-American female writer described how a white male mentor helped early in her career:

I wrote a script for *Little House on the Prairie* that was given to an agent who liked it, who signed me...they got me my first job, which was writing for the

Little House on the Prairie episode and it was the best possible initiation into writing TV in this city, I think, because of working for Michael Landon who considered himself a minority in that he considered himself a Jewish male who had been discriminated against. He had a certain identity to helping me because he felt a certain kinship about that, isn't that unusual? Interesting.

She recognized the irony in her situation: receiving assistance from a white, Jewish male, precisely the type of individual accused by writers of practicing discrimination against minorities.

There were other positive remarks. One individual portrayed "a guy who was really my godfather, Herb Schlosser, we were really close. [Grant] Tinker hired me and gave me the shot then Tinker leaves and Schlosser came out to take his place and Schlosser was the guy, I've really got to say, who recognized whatever abilities I had and pushed me up, real fast."

Successful female writers also served as mentors for minority writers, primarily women, in Hollywood. The names of writer-producers such as Diane English, Linda Bloodworth-Thomason and Barbara Corday frequently surfaced when individuals discussed help they received. Ironically, the same Barbara Corday was also accused, by a male minority writer of practicing discrimination.

This inconsistency illustrates a larger problem occurring among minority writers. Individuals repeatedly contradicted themselves and one another when describing their experiences with Hollywood's white establishment. In addition, minority writers expressed gratitude towards specific individuals but condemned Anglos or the "white establishment" as a group.

Faced with reconciling their mistrust of the Hollywood establishment with a history of receiving help from various mentors, minorities resolved this conflict awkwardly, claiming that the majority individuals who helped them were exceptions. Even certain mentors received a mixed response; Norman Lear was a case in point.

The mere mention of Lear's name elicited reactions from members of every minority group represented. Opinions were diverse and extreme. Because he has openly sought their creative input, talents, and—according to some—played "kingmaker," Lear has left himself vulnerable to minority criticism and hostility. However, even when attacking him, minorities acknowledged Lear's power. Several writers were extremely critical of how Lear's former company, Tandem

Productions (now Embassy Productions), had skirted the Writers Guild requirement that each episodic television show have one minority writer on staff. In one instance Tandem claimed they had satisfied the requirement after they bought an idea from a black school teacher originally hired to tutor the show's underage actors. One writer who had participated in an organized protest against Tandem's practices expressed a grudging admiration of their ruse and remarked, "I'd still like to work for that son of a bitch someday."

Lear was characterized by many as the quintessential kingmaker, able to make or break careers. An African-American woman writer explained how a black producer, "who's just an excellent writer but...has a very eccentric personality," was helped by Lear, who overlooked the man's personal peculiarities and informed his associates, "You're going to give this guy a job on the show whether you like it or not." According to this writer, Lear's protégé "now...has a reputation where he can go wherever he wants to." In another "kingmaker" tale a minority writer related, the coda was not as satisfactory:

Now there are situations where guys have gone in and gotten a leg up from the company and done very good. Michael Maurier's over at Embassy, which was Tandem Productions. Norman Lear brought him in, but Norman brought him in almost as a slap in the face to the writers who were in town. He took him right out of school in the south and immediately made him story editor on one of the shows and took him on as an apprentice and said, "I can teach him better than anyone here because I'm in the business." So he sort of put him in and Michael was doing *The Jeffersons* and even when they made him producer of the show, he was not allowed to hire any writing talent. He was so paranoid about it that they had to put a buffer between him and them because he was not in a position to hire any blacks...That's what Lear's done and it's blatantly racist.

Other incidents involving Lear have had complicated and negative outcomes. One writer explained:

Look at Eric Monty. A long time ago he had created *What's Happening?* Now that was a career high for him. Eric was over in Norman Lear's operation. They had sworn to Eric that...they would let him direct some episodes of the show and they would put him on as a story editor and they kept dangling the carrot. They never let him direct the thing and what not and finally Eric sued Norman. Well, as a result of that, Eric was dropped from Tandem and every other show and can't get a job and that's crazy. I mean anyone else who has a show on TV that's running in syndication can find work anywhere. Not Eric Monty. The same thing with Bob Peete. After Bob Peete had a job with Norman, he was out of work six years. He was associate producer on four of Norman's shows, including *All in the Family*. Everyone else on that show had an immediate development deal they went right into it. But not Bob. Think about the waste of talent!

This latter grievance—the lack of future development deals—arose in discussions with writers of underrepresented groups. However, unlike previous accusations directed at the Hollywood establishment, these cases specify Lear as personally responsible for the failure of minority writers to advance.

So many stories concerning Lear circulated among minority writers that it was difficult to separate valid accounts from idle gossip. Several minority writers attributed a quote to Lear in which he allegedly stated that there were no qualified black writers in Hollywood. Its familiarity notwithstanding, this story was easily disputed. Lear is acknowledged as having hired—at one time or another—a large number of the African-American writers employed in the entertainment industry. In light of this, his dismissing the talents of all black writers in Hollywood does not make sense.

The critique of Lear took more extreme forms. A Latino writer's evaluation of Lear's professional conduct ultimately deteriorated into character assassination:

Well, Norman Lear has an excellent public relations man because here's a man who made an incredible amount of money and a reputation from black-white confrontation and yet he had to be forced to hire black writers because he did not do it on his own, and yet now, he's credited for being the first one who hired African-American writers but it didn't come out of him, someone had to force him to do it. I was there when Redd Foxx walked off the set and left because there were no black writers. This was years ago—ancient history—I was real young and I'm asking, "Aren't there any black writers?" And, of course, it doesn't occur to you, it takes a while for people to put two and two together. You look around, you see all these faces and you wonder whether maybe the writing is being done behind closed doors someplace and you just don't know about it, you're left out. But even other African-Americans now, I hear people like Keenan Ivory Wayans saying that Norman Lear was the first, the father of black writers. They don't know the history. No one has really written anything about this, no one really knows. I mean the man is a big hypocrite and I mean I am not afraid to say it on this thing [tape recorder] because I don't like him...I understand he has to be medicated...he's on lithium.

Often such personal attacks backfired, undercutting the credibility of minority writers, rather than Norman Lear. Still, when numerous writers related the same or similar anecdotes, it was difficult to question their reliability. Repeated with conviction, the stories involving Lear—among others—began to take on a life of their own. One anecdote was repeated by four minority writers, all with different backgrounds. Having gone unquestioned, this story has passed into minority legend. One writer offered his version, recalling, "I was in a meeting with Norman once and he was sitting there and he said, 'Now here's what happens when a black family gets around the table.' I said, 'How many black families have you had dinner with?'" Lear has never remarked on these supposed incidents nor refuted minority charges.

While some of the more extreme remarks can be attributed to rage and frustration, the sheer volume of incidents reported that involve Lear prevents minority claims of discrimination and unfair treatment from being taken lightly. Whether they indicate impropriety on Lear's part or self-defeating misperceptions of minority writers, the meaning of these claims must be considered.

What ultimately emerged was a picture of minority discomfort at the control one individual exercised over their personal and professional aspirations. Although they evoked gratitude, Lear's efforts to develop minority talent were suspected and resented. He was certainly not a hero; a white father-figure was probably the last identity object minorities desired. The resentment of Lear was consistent and palpable; the transference negative. He may embody what minorities fear most in Hollywood: their lack of control over their own fate.

Norman Lear was not the only object of minority hostility. The minority backlash against majority powers defined other, larger targets. Frustrated with their inability to succeed and their own lack of control, minority writers have identified a scapegoat responsible for their difficulties in Hollywood.

Anti-Semitism

To a certain extent, minority writers blamed the entire white establishment of Hollywood for their problems, claiming discrimination was practiced industry wide. Still, when questioned concerning who or what created the greatest obstacles to their success in Hollywood, minorities invariably answered "the Jews." The Jews were perceived as controlling power and positions in the entertainment industry. Writers insisted Hollywood was a "Jewish town" where, in order to succeed, an individual had to be Jewish. Or, as one minority writer lamented, only slightly tongue-in-cheek, "I shouldn't have gone to AFI, I should have gone to synagogue."

The hostility towards Jews that minority writers expressed was startling in its openness and its consistency. Writers with different ethnic backgrounds all indicted the Jews for practicing discrimination. White Jewish males were characterized as only being interested in helping other Jews, otherwise being anti-black, anti-Latin, or generally anti-minority in their sentiments and unwilling to help other groups. According to one writer:

You see one of the problems is it's an old boys' network and all the studios...go to people they know. And most of them are Jewish and you know, people don't understand when they talk about the schism between the blacks, the Jews, it's on a security level. Blacks say, "*Why?* Who are they? Who anointed them to be the rulers of this business?" It's tough. You try not to be racist, or display any religious prejudice but when you start looking at the figures and who does and who does not work, and people say, "Well, we are on your side, we're with you!" Well, okay, fine, do something then, do something!! I think Spike Lee is one of the people who's blown the top off this whole thing and I, for one, am glad he did.

Another individual named white executives and producers with reputations for supporting liberal causes in the community and insisted each was racist and discriminated against minorities. This writer revealed that he kept documents on specific people, particularly the Jews he felt impeded minority success. He identified Barbara Corday, a successful writer, producer, and former studio executive as a bigot, explaining that a young African-American male who applied for a staff position and presented an ideal résumé and qualifications was dismissed by Corday out of personal bias rather than professional objectivity. He then stated that friends were aware he kept the man's résumé with Corday's comments in his safe. In the event he was ever "in trouble" he would produce this damning document.

His remarks were extreme. Most minority writers tried to tie their anti-Semitism to reality, explaining their anger at the Jews by drawing on their own experience. However, there were a few individuals whose rage appeared inexhaustible. One minority writer was notorious for being outspoken in her antipathy towards the Jews. When interviewed, she denounced the Jewish conspiracy against minorities and then launched into a litany of stereotypes traditionally used to deprecate Jews, claiming their devotion to money and financial gain overrode all else, including their concern for family and personal relationships. Other writers who expressed animosity towards the Jews were quick to state that this writer was extreme in her judgment. One writer even ridiculed her for the irrationality of her views. The individuals who were excessive in their criticism of the Jews were well known to other writers and discounted as unrealistic or disturbed. But even more temperate writers insisted, "the Jews *do* control the networks."

In contrast, certain successful minorities credited Jewish writers and producers with helping them achieve a foothold in the industry. But again, minority writers viewed these individuals as exceptions. In general, Jewish writers and producers stirred resentment, even from individuals they tried to help. Despite good intentions and liberal sensibilities, the Jews' efforts to identify with and help minority writers met with resistance and criticism. Minorities did not accept the Jews' argument that they—along with African-Americans, Latinos, Asians, women, etc.—were an underrepresented group, encountering the same discrimination in majority culture. Several writers stated that despite Jewish claims of sharing fates with other minorities, their true prejudice and insensitivity eventually emerged. In one instance a writer recalled:

Sometimes they would be talking around the room like we weren't there, making jokes about black people and [saying] "Don't be so sensitive, we're only kidding, you can talk about Jews." I said, "Well, you know, that's not my personality. I don't want to talk about Jews, I don't want to make racial slurs about Jews, is that okay with you?" Those were the things we had to deal with. And one day, we were sitting in a story conference, the executive producer said—and he fooled me because I thought he was being sincere for a little while—he said, "...you know when we talk about the cast, do you really think we're talking about black people?" So we said, "Yeah." And so he said, "Well, I don't want you to feel that way because it's not true, we're just talking about actors in general and they're morons. And I don't want you to feel uncomfortable because when you are uncomfortable, you make me uncomfortable and then I feel I have to censor myself and that is stifling me creatively." I thought to myself, "Well, he is just bullshitting me, in other words he is telling me to shut up." So I just ignored it and then I figured out he was just bullshitting because he said, "Well, give me an example of when you think I've said something racist?" So I brought up a few instances where he had used the word nigger and other things and I mean, he used to say this!! Imagine what it was like for me and he would say it in a joking manner and add, "It means nothing if you can call me Jewboy, you can call me kike." So anyway, I brought up the instances and we went through this long discussion and I just finally said, "Forget it. All I want to do is get through the rest of the season and then I don't want to see you anymore. I don't care if I am out of work."

Minorities viewed Jewish control extending into other areas. The Jews were held responsible not only for the absence of ethnic minorities from Hollywood, but also for the lack of minority-oriented projects in the industry. Minority writers voiced many complaints concerning creative territory. They insisted that because Jews control the entertainment industry, television and film are devoted largely to the Jewish experience. One minority writer criticized what he considered the oversupply of monies and television programs on the Holocaust and the shortage of minority projects. He then shifted his criticism to the inappropriateness of Jewish writers claiming they were qualified to work on projects with minority themes:

I got into a big argument with...a producer once who came in to see me with a black story when I was at the network and he said, "Well, this is really the way blacks are." I said, "Oh." He said, "I think I know a little more than you." I said, "Wait a minute, let me ask you a question; you're Jewish?" He said, "Yeah." I said, "How would you feel if I came in here and said I'm going to do the definitive story on the Holocaust." He said, "Well, you can't know about that, you're not Jewish." I said, "You don't understand what you just said and I don't want to talk to you." Because they do that, they come in and they say they know and if a black writer comes in with a white idea, they look down on him.

Several minority writers advanced a double standard in relation to creative territory. They rejected Jewish writers' claims to minority status along with the idea that Jews were qualified to write about the minority experience. Ethnic minority writers felt only they could validly interpret their own experience, they were the only witnesses. At the same time, minorities claimed they could write about white experience more effectively than the Jews. Many claimed that Jews understood their own experience, an area that had received adequate coverage. This left Jewish writers with little creative territory of their own.

It is clear that most minority writers perceived the Jews as adversaries. However, by focusing on the Jews, these minority writers have ignored changes in the organization of Hollywood. The entertainment industry was originally built through the efforts of Jewish immigrants eager to amass fortunes and create dynasties (see Gabler 1988). However, the "old Hollywood" of authoritarian moguls and studio autocracy has vanished with the composition of the industry drastically altered. Hollywood is now controlled largely by conglomerates and diversified corporations, who count the entertainment industry as one of many divisions. McClintick's (1982) exposé of the David Begelman-Columbia Pictures scandal and Bach's (1985) account of United Artists' *Heaven's Gate* debacle demonstrated the corporate influences of Wall Street and TransAmerica Corporation respectively. Additionally, the Japanese takeover of three studios in the past five years has significantly altered the power structure of Hollywood. Despite this and other proof of corporate power in Hollywood, many minority writers ignored who exerted control in Hollywood, although some individual exceptions were more sophisticated in their understandings.[2]

In the end, it was still "the Jews" who were blamed for discrimination and other obstacles minority writers encountered. The projection of responsibility was strong and dramatic, underlining minority writers' perception that they did not control their own fate. The Jews of the Hollywood establishment provided minorities with an outlet for frustration and a scapegoat for rage. In turn, the behavior of many white Jewish males may have been far from exemplary. The consequences of this conflict are troublesome. Minority writers feel increasingly estranged from the Hollywood establishment who, unaffected by anti-Semitism, interpreted the hostility and rage as a sign that minorities are unable to function in the entertainment industry.

Rationale

Minority writers needed to make sense of their inability to achieve lasting success in Hollywood. The problem of discrimination was difficult for writers to confront and their explanations combine an objective assessment of reality with a subjective assignment of blame. In certain instances, minority writers understood situations, evaluating their outcome accurately. However, all too often what appeared to be an explanation was actually a defense. In general, the more minority writers avoided acknowledging their role in the situation, the more suspect their reasoning.

The most frequent explanation for discrimination involved minority writers' claim that the Hollywood establishment was simply more comfortable working with writers who shared their backgrounds. Or, as one writer succinctly explained, "To be a writer you've got to be short and Jewish." Certain individuals insisted the majority attitude was more a personal preference than an objective evaluation of quality. One minority writer asserted that given three writers of equal ability with equally good works, the writer most likely to be hired would be "white, Jewish, and male," simply because he matched characteristics with the individuals doing the hiring. Another writer went so far as to state that many producers and executives actually liked minority writers personally but had "set ideas" as to what writers should be, namely, "mirror images of themselves." One African-American female writer elaborated, "It is much, much easier for a white male to make it in this town. Why? Well, again, it's people that are looking for someone who's like you—that's who I feel most comfortable with, someone who is like me. These people who are running Hollywood are not women, they are not minorities, they are white men and that's who they are going to look to help out and it's not easy to get around."

This phrase "most comfortable" cropped up over and over again as minority writers discussed majority discrimination. Minority writers were convinced that their fear of differences prevented the industry establishment from working with minorities. Minority writers were not unsympathetic: many proposed that the Hollywood establishment was entrapped by its own unconscious bias and uncertainty.

Not surprisingly, others were more extreme in their views. A few writers claimed that the minority presence threatened Hollywood powers. These writers reasoned that white Jewish writers and producers did not want to share control. "You know they didn't want blacks to play baseball or basketball either and then we took over and if these jokers are not careful, before they know it, we will have taken over...They're afraid of losing control." Perhaps the idea that minorities posed a threat to majority power appealed to individuals who believed they had little control over their own fates.

Using a different explanation, certain minority writers located the cause of discrimination in structural factors. These writers eschewed questions of individual comfort and control, concentrating on how the structure of Hollywood in particular or society in general thwarted minority accomplishment. These individuals felt minority writers had little to offer in the system of patronage and symbiotic obligation that characterized the entertainment industry. One writer explained:

Hollywood is a town of doing favors. A lot of times, someone will help you out because they think down the line you will be able to do a favor for them and it's also in a lot of the minds of these people—older people especially—that there is nothing that a minority can do for me. I might be able to do something for him, but what can he do for me down the line? The chances are very slim of him making it, so why waste my time with somebody like that. There could be something we could do for you down the line, but a lot of people aren't willing to take that chance. They think they'll stick their necks out and get nothing in return—or maybe even trouble.

Discrimination was implicit in the conduct of everyday life in Hollywood. Unfortunately, minorities claimed that because of majority bias they were unable to achieve positions or power that would enable them to compete adequately in the Hollywood marketplace where mutual backscratching is not simply advisable but essential.

The apparent inescapability of discrimination forced several writers into far-reaching appraisals of the minority predicament that extended beyond Hollywood to encompass modern social organization. It was not simply the entertainment industry that was biased but society in general. In discussing the injustice and intolerance one writer was explicit that for minorities trying to succeed in Hollywood was

Very difficult, extremely difficult. Because it is a racist society. Not just the motion picture industry, but we live in a racist society, a racist and sexist society, and Hollywood is part of that. I can remember when I finished college, I went looking for a job and I went to Paramount. The woman at Paramount tells me, "Well, I can't hire you because if I did, I'd have to hire another colored person for you to have somebody to talk to." It was kind of pervasive, racism, in the industry at the time. I sometimes wonder if it's changed at all.

Similarly, other minority writers indicted not only the entertainment industry but all of American society. The extent of their accusation was matched by the depth of their frustration.

Discrimination in the entertainment industry is an everyday reality for most minority writers. It informs their work and their professional concerns. The emotional pain minority writers experience affects their perception of Hollywood and their interaction with industry members. As one writer stated, with resignation:

I have tried. I've seen people try every approach from bringing guns and knives, literally, to just saying, "Screw it." But the sad part about it is that there is really nothing you can do about it. It breaks people apart, because you even are reluctant to form friendships because you know you are not going to be able to continue to work that way. You know in a way that you have to enjoy working with someone because they are not going to give you a chance to do it again.

Story Telling

To make sense of their experience in Hollywood, many minority writers told stories, often in elaborate detail. As they described their responses to discrimination and their experiences in Hollywood, this story telling served as an outlet for rage and frustration. However, story telling functioned as more than a form of emotional release. These narratives eased disappointment but they also criticized, advised, and warned.

In general, the stories contained the message that underrepresented groups were ignored, shortchanged, or exploited by the Hollywood establishment. Understandably, the specifics of the story depended on the narrator's identity, but the general themes of minority perseverance and virtue contrasted with majority insensitivity and ignorance, which always predominated. In these accounts, minorities invariably emerged as understanding and, at times, secure, while industry figures appeared as callous in their treatment of minorities and frightened about their own futures.

Certain stories were told by several writers. One anecdote involved how majority individuals inappropriately claimed to understand the minority experience. One writer related his version:

Some lady executive, when Alex Haley was doing *Palmerstown* had the nerve to say at this conference that Gordon Berry and I went to, she said, "I had to tell Alex Haley about, I had to explain to him about the black family." This was at an open meeting and people got up and booed. They said, "How dare you!" Tony Brown tore her up because he was on the same panel. He said, "That was the worst comment, you had to tell Alex Haley about the black family? How dare *you*?" And she had the nerve to say it and believe it. That's one of the things about the industry and these people, 'cause most of them don't realize how racist they really are.

This story resembled another anecdote featuring Norman Lear in place of the anonymous executive.

While many narratives revolved around themes of creativity and expertise, stereotyping was also a frequent topic. The two combined in one individual's account of an attempt to expunge a negative stereotype from an episode of *Miami Vice*:

In this one particular incident it was something that I had seen in script form that initially, instinctively, bothered me and I said, "Well, let's see how they shoot it," because again you never know how a director is going to shoot something and I don't want to inhibit the creative process, that's the other thing you have to say. So although my initial instinct was "Wow!—Am I being overly sensitive?" or "Well, let's see how they shoot it." Sat in dailies and saw the film that day, I said, "Oh I was right! This is terrible, this can't happen." Got on the phone and called up the guy [in charge]. He said, "Well, gee, you know it was such an insignificant role that I didn't even realize it but I think you're right and let me get on it and see what we can do to change it, okay?" And what it was, was the guys were searching down a lead and they happen to go to a drug den where everybody is in there shooting up drugs and this guy is looking for his source and he finds this lady, she happened to be a black woman and she is sitting on a crate strung out on drugs and he's offering her some more drugs to get this information and by way of introduction he says, "Ah, Linda, you're out of work again," and she said, "Yeah, the law, law is a bummer." She's an attorney...it bothered me so much and when I saw it shot I just knew how wrong it was because it is the only time we see this lady, we never see her again, it's totally out of context and to me it was saying to young people out there, you know, why pursue a college education, degree, and become a lawyer? It's not worth it, you'll just end up shooting drugs anyway...this young black woman with a syringe in her arm, telling kids out there, "I don't need the aggravation of being a lawyer!!"...I stopped it... Everybody said, "Wow, yeah, you're right!!"...but I mean this was an instance of...what to me was a glaring thing and nobody noticed it, nobody noticed it. But then you point a finger at it and they said, "Gee, I think you're right about that."

Still other stories focused on problems minorities faced trying to "break in" to Hollywood. One Latino writer related a lengthy tale concerning a celebrity who promised to help minorities with their struggle:

...when the Latino Writers Group in the Writers Guild had their first thing and Anthony Quinn was their guest of honor and everybody was so afraid and so intimidated by *the* Anthony Quinn...and here he is and we're all shaking...at the end he comes up to me and says, "You do writing?" "Yeah." He says, "Okay, send me your stuff." And he turns to the women and says, "Hey, get my man a pencil here," and as the women are running all over the place trying to find pencils for Anthony Quinn he says, "You tell them that Anthony Quinn says anything you write, I'll be in." Of course he didn't do anything and that's not the answer. That's not it [not the way to gain access]. It's somehow being in the right place with the right script, that's what stops you. It just never happens—Anthony Quinn can't help.

Minority writers enjoyed debunking fame as part of the story-telling process. Celebrities who made empty gestures figured in many narratives, including one story involving a well-known actor-producer-director:

Warren Beatty was once at the Writers Guild, the biggest pompous ass who ever walked...they had let a few of us "Open Door" people in and they kept saying this and that and they always give you the same kreplach, which is, "We want good stories, we are always looking for good stories and good writers." So this one kid stands up and says, "Excuse me a minute." They wouldn't let him talk—they said, "Are you a Guild member?" "No, he's not a Guild member," "Ah, sit down." So finally he persists, so one of the liberals got up and said, "Okay, I want to ask a question and it's his question and I am a Guild member and I have been present at the Guild and he wants to know how you get a script in." And he [Beatty] says, "Look, I've got thousands of scripts coming in, I just made a big hit. He's going to have to come up with some innovative way for me to get the script and if he can't come up with it, then I don't need him." Okay, he put the kid down. Okay, next couple of weeks I hear that at the Writers Guild

Theater, the old celebrity theater on Melrose, there's a celebrity parking lot that held about eight or ten cars. Warren Beatty had his Mercedes out there, whatever he is driving. The kid comes up with a script, goes up to Warren Beatty and says, "Excuse me, Mr. Beatty," and he pulls out a switchblade and puts it to his neck and says, "Could you please read my script?" and Warren Beatty said, "Be more than happy to."

Stories served as both an explanation and a defense. They allowed minority writers to rationalize their difficulties, enabling them to overcome feelings of disillusion and betrayal. By telling stories minority writers also shared an esprit de corps; individuals discovered they were not alone in their experiences of disappointment. Also, story telling empowered minority writers to perpetuate a mythology in which they emerged as heroes with the Hollywood establishment as villains or, worse still, fools.

Talent and the Response to Discrimination
There was, however, one issue minority writers did not discuss: talent. No one considered whether some minority writers did not succeed in Hollywood because their work was unacceptable. Instead, minorities claimed their access was blocked by industry bias and fear. They insisted their rejection by Hollywood was due to the practice of discrimination rather than the absence of talent. Minority writers insisted their abilities matched those of white male writers. Some acknowledged progress was being made. Altogether, minority writers displayed both emotional and strategic plans to respond to the problem of discrimination.

Notes

[1] Every writer interviewed reported encountering some form of discrimination while working in Hollywood with two exceptions. One writer, a physically challenged Latino screenwriter reported precisely the opposite experience. Producers actually failed to make appropriate allowances for his disability:

I haven't even noticed any uncomfortableness with whether or not I can take a certain project on. I have had producers actually expect more out of me than I was capable of doing and I kind of had to tell them. I am still getting psychologically prepared for plane travel and so on and I have one producer ready to send me to New York and so basically the ignorance I encounter is more in my favor.

This writer, recently disabled, also explained that he had, at one point, thought that his disability would encourage producers and directors to work with him, as a "feather in their cap." He revised this idea, although it is unclear why.

The second writer interviewed announced when asked if he had felt discriminated against:

No, never, never, never!! I think that it's something that you make up in your mind. It's almost like fear in animals. If you are an animal and you sense that another animal has fear, you will become a predator upon that animal...The same thing with being a minority. If you think that you are a minority and if you think that people are going to be prejudiced because you are ethnic, people will pick up on that and kind of look at you funny because you don't quite fit in. But if you think that you're not a minority and that you're just like they are and you've got things in common...you don't have any problems from the other person. It's when you go out of your way to be different and to be like part of your heritage and all that, then people will treat you different...if you treat yourself like an outsider, you become that.

²One black female writer actually specified that, at one studio, all powerful executives had offices located above a certain floor in the main office building.

Chapter Seven

✦ ✦ ✦

The Response to Discrimination

Minority writers responded to the problems discrimination engendered. Their reactions, both constructive and destructive, affected everyone involved in the entertainment industry. To understand their current status in Hollywood, it helps to review the relationship between minorities and the Writers Guild. In 1977, minority groups were first recognized as warranting Guild attention. Special recommendations for minority writers were outlined in Article Number 38 of the Writers Guild Members' Basic Agreement. At the time, these recommendations concerned one minority group: black writers. In 1981, Article 38 was updated to include other groups. Instead of one general minority committee, several committees would represent the interests of specific protected classes. Difficulties immediately arose concerning the definition of a "protected class." It was decided that protected classes were those groups of writers encountering employment difficulties for reasons other than writing capability: Women, Blacks, Hispanics, Native American and Asian-Pacific writers. At an April 1986 Board meeting, writers over 40 years old and writers with physical disabilities were also designated as protected classes on the basis of discrimination they encountered.

The Guild then moved forward on a data submission program to collect information on the employment of the protected classes. A statistical study was commissioned by the Writers Guild, West, to examine employment opportunities and activities of its members. The report, completed by William T. Bielby and Denise Bielby, focused on differences between four groups of writers: white males, females, minorities, and writers over the age of 40.[1]

Submitted on June 16, 1987, the report indicated the following overall trends:

1) Just over half (54 percent) of all Guild members were employed at some time during 1985.

2) From January 1982 through December 1985, white males accounted for almost 80 percent of the employed WGAW writers. Women comprised just under 20 percent of employed WGAW writers, and minorities made up about 2 percent of employed writers each year.

3) There is tremendous variation across production companies in the propensity to employ women, minorities, and older writers and in the pay differentials between these groups and white male writers.

4) The television and feature film industry provides few employment opportunities for minority writers, pays women and minority writers between 60 to 70 cents for every dollar earned by white males, and increasingly values younger writers in both pay and employment opportunities.

5) Despite the fact that much writing for television is compensated at Guild minimums, there are two mechanisms through which white male writers can earn considerably more than females, minorities, and older writers. First, white male writers can obtain *more* work than other groups primarily through more writing assignments and writing for longer programs. Second, white males are more often employed in *better-paying* work than other groups, including staff positions, pilot and development deals, and writing the final script instead of less lucrative original stories. Women and minorities are more often cut off at story level.

6) Women are less likely than men to be employed as staff writers for television. Minority writers have greater difficulty than non-minority writers in obtaining freelance employment in television. Minority television writers are concentrated on the staffs of a few series that have minority actors in leading or feature roles.

7) Barriers to employment faced by women, minorities, and writers over the age of 40 are greater in feature film, especially at the major studios, than in television.

8) The most striking statistical finding is that white male writers have an earnings advantage in every sector of the industry: at the majors, independents, networks, smaller companies, in both feature film and television.

These findings were important to the Guild and to minority writers as a record of what occurred in the entertainment industry. Finally, numerically operationalized, the experiences of minority writers and people of color were demonstrated to the Guild and to the powerful of Hollywood. Follow-up studies since 1987 have shown that little has changed.

Minorities and the Writers Guild

Most minority writers participated in Writers Guild programs with varying degrees of involvement and satisfaction. Their strong and definite opinions of the Guild and its activities were, for the most part, unfavorable. One writer explained that "part of the problem with the Writers Guild is that there are always going to be frustrated people because there are too many writers in Hollywood. There are just not enough jobs to go around, not even a thousand, there's not even 220. I think that someone had figured out how many assignments there were— 169 or something. So there is always going to be some frustration that you are going to have to deal with but, still, there are people that you are leaving out more than others and those people have to be dealt with eventually, one way or another, it's going to happen."

Many writers maintained that the Guild failed to address issues crucial to minorities and people of color, characterizing the Guild as an organization that responded mainly to its predominantly white male membership. One African-American writer declared the Guild was operated by male Jewish writers as a "closed shop," thwarting minority efforts in Hollywood while placating them with affirmative action committees and special programs. "The problem with the Guild," he explained, "is that the Guild is a very racist, a very sexist organization. They just want a certain few people to make it...They are not interested 'cause they know, those old Jews know that, hey, if we get a few more young people working here, more people of color and more women, it'll cut into us and they don't want that to happen."

"You think that writers historically are big liberals," another writer remarked, "but the Guild is not that strong, it's not that liberal. There are a few people in the Guild that way, but most of them are minority voices."

In general, minorities viewed majority writers as the lackeys of the Hollywood establishment, a view with questionable validity. "The Writers Guild is made up of old hand-servants," one writer commented, "and they're not going to do anything outside of the norm." If these white writers gained any power in Hollywood, becoming producers or directors, they were accused of practicing discrimination against their minority counterparts. One African-American writer outlined the inconsistency of the situation, observing, "You know on the one hand you have to say it's not really the Guild's fault [the lack of minority employment] although one of the issues that I haven't really considered that's been brought up is that most of the people who hire writers, story editors, and producers, are really writers. They *are* members of the Guild you see, so the Guild does have a certain amount of culpability in terms of it has made no effort to sensitize their own membership to the fact that they are discriminating."

In many ways, the Writers Guild was also held indirectly responsible for discriminating against minorities. One writer revealed discrimination inherent in Guild policy:

They have this whole thing where they retire you, if you don't sell. First you are a full-fledged member, then you are an associate member and then if you don't sell anything over a number of seasons, they just retire you out to pasture and most blacks, almost all the blacks I know, have been put out to pasture, because they don't get work. You just basically get kicked out of the union. And so you know, the woman that's the head of the Women's Committee is saying that it's really disgusting, because we are trying to fight and help, and you [referring to herself] can't even be involved because you're like outside of it!

Special Programs

Despite these attacks, the Writers Guild attempted to carry out an equal opportunity mandate. To accomplish their stated aim of improving minority writers' position in the industry, the Guild established two special programs for protected class writers: the Script Submission Program and the Writers Training Program.

The Script Submission Program required the major studios and production companies to accept scripts from members of the protected classes, except for writers over 40 years old.[2] Writers were told that they did not need agents or experience and it was hoped that such an arrangement would foster increased production of minority scripts. After an initial flurry of activity, however, the program grew quiescent. Scripts were submitted and, according to one minority writer, "never looked at."

As the unreviewed scripts accumulated the situation became "totally nightmarish." In addition, studio response to the program was extremely negative. According to a guild assistant, "they don't mince words when it comes to the quality of the scripts." Most studios claimed the scripts submitted to them were inadequate and the Guild assistant added, "the success rate was not all that terrific. We sent them in but the studios just didn't respond. I think two of the scripts submitted were read, but the rest were ignored."

In contrast, the Guild experienced considerably more success with its special training programs. Article 38 of the Writers Guild Agreement established the Writers Training Program, requiring production companies, networks, and studios to provide one staff position for a protected class member. In addition, various studios, under the auspices of the Guild, organized additional "Open Door" programs to train minority writers and facilitate their future employment in Hollywood. Over half the minority writers interviewed participated in these euphemistically labeled undertakings. The programs resembled internships, offering minorities staff experience for a defined time period at a reduced salary. Additionally, some programs provided direct instruction in writing techniques and general skills useful to Hollywood writers.

Minorities successfully completed these programs, although their reactions varied. Many individuals responded positively, claiming the programs provided an unexpected opportunity, aiding access and encouraging their continued writing. For several, the programs enhanced their university or film school background. One black female writer explained:

Many minority writers, blacks in particular, who are working in the industry, were trained in that writers' program and everyone had different backgrounds and many of us had come from academic backgrounds where writing was part of the curriculum but this was geared more towards writing for the industry and being able to not only write but market what you've written cause that's equally as important as writing in this business. Because of that program and the connections it gave me, I sold my first script. It was wonderful.

Another writer observed that "the programs were organized when people were still saying, 'Let's see what we can do to help minorities become a part of things.' And so there was still a great deal of social conscience and a lot of people helped me, I think, men helped me, white males helped me a lot."

Most positive remarks concerning the "Open Door" program were made by women writers. Their appreciation may partly be related to their continued success once their participation ended. One Latino writer described her excitement, recalling, "I can see myself ten years ago, when I was just beginning, when I was taking those classes and stuff, getting into 'the situation'...at Universal, going as an apprentice writer and meeting the producers of the world and exchanging ideas with them and having them say, 'That's a lousy idea but you've got something there, go back and work on it some more and when you figure out what to do with that, then come back and see me.' It was great. I never thought I would be where I am today."

In lauding the special programs, women writers emphasized their feelings of acceptance and the value of creative feedback. However, other writers expressed ambivalence or openly criticized the minority programs. One writer remembered when he "got into this program. They didn't give me an office, they didn't give me anywhere to sit so I had to sit in the line producer's office all day long in a chair. They had nothing for me to do. I mean, I was an affirmative action number, they had nothing for me to do. And I didn't learn anything." Another African-American writer questioned the actual motives of the white establishment:

Now I suspect that they got a good deal out of that, in teaching a class of minorities and listening to the views of minorities at the same time they are teaching. It certainly helped break up their old ways of thinking about certain things, listen to new ideas, new insights, which you can use in your own writing so that there it worked both ways, I'm sure. The minorities, on the other hand, got the opportunity to talk to professional writers, something you don't get normally in a classroom situation so some of these minorities, because of that, made friends with some of these writers and later on were able to become members of the Guild as a result of that, not many. I was one.

Many minority writers revived the argument that such special programs represented token efforts to defuse minority anger without offering any substantial opportunity. One writer recalled:

One particular very successful production company in town had some sort of a minority writers program that they were touting around town as really trying to help by having some shows that deal with minority needs and many of them have been quite successful...Anyway, I went and met with the man who was running the program. A black guy, and he told me "off the record" that I'm wasting my time 'cause they [writers, producers, executives] are not trying to help anybody, they are not going to give anybody any kind of program or get anybody into the industry but it's part of what they need to do for their image because I guess that complaints had been made about them, here they are making so much money off of these ethnic shows and they are not doing anything and they hardly had any minority writers working on any of the shows, so...That was just typical. And they had helped a few people. There had been a couple of people that I know of who actually got involved in the program and went to work and wrote TV—but those were the minority of the minority...you can't have a program and not have *anyone* ever come through it and anything or you would be obvious to everyone that it's a joke so you have to have that one or two tokens that you can point to and say, "Well, look at what we've done." But that was one of the better ones. Most of them haven't even done that.

Other writers ridiculed industry efforts and repeated claims that special "Open Door" programs existed to assuage white guilt. This ultimately engendered further resentment. "So often the jobs are gotten mainly through some sort of sense of guilt or through some sort of pressure that's placed on people," a writer commented. "The problem is, if I had a business, I wouldn't care what it was, and someone came in, some group, whoever it was and forced someone, an employee on me, regardless of right or wrong or whatever the issue is, I am going to resent that and that employee will probably never go very far in my organization, just because of the way...that they were brought in there."

Individuals railed that these programs were another form of discrimination experienced writers were forced to endure because they were the only job opportunities available to minorities in Hollywood. Probably the most extensive and objective critique of all the special programs was offered by one physically challenged writer, who explained:

I have a lot of questions about the special programs. They do not really make sense. It does not address the need. And the basic reason that it doesn't address the need is the attitude of the people who drafted the [Writers Guild] agreement is if you are not white and under 40 and male, then obviously you need training to become a full fledged member of the Guild. The training isn't the issue. We've got 70 black writers with college degrees as screenwriters. We've got women in the Guild who have been there for 40 years and have been working for years. They don't need training, they don't need to have scripts submitted under a training program. "The Open Door Program" is considered to be the most successful minority program the Guild has ever had in that a lot of writers who went through the Open Door got work. My question is do they get work because of the Open Door or do they get work because they were Guild members and they were making great contacts? And that's not been addressed. The white writers on the [Writers Guild] board currently who worked with the Open Door feel that's the true way of dealing with affirmative action and the Minority Committees say, "We don't need training, we've been in the Guild for ten years, we sell our scripts, we have agents, we don't need a training program." They do not need training, they need jobs, they need access.

His remarks were underscored by an African-American writer who depicted how she and the Hollywood establishment worked at cross purposes, stating, "For me it was access first, access. But always always, always, they wanted to put me in a training program. If they ever said anything to me it was a training program."

Minority writers displayed complex and mixed reaction to the special programs. Because of this, the program's impact was difficult to evaluate. One writer went so far as to describe the courses as "desperately humiliating," and even participants who portrayed the program in glowing terms have not necessarily made continuous progress in the industry. But most successful minority writers were participants.

In addition, these programs served an unanticipated function: minorities were further identified as a group separate from the mainstream, to be treated as a a special case, needing help. Despite endorsement, the stigma of "separate and not equal" shadowed these arrangements. Despite their possible effectiveness, minority problems remain.

The Writers Guild is in a difficult position, operating with marginal effectiveness. In attempting to placate minorities, serve its white majority, and satisfy the industry establishment, it may actually thwart efforts at exposing discrimination. One black female writer described what would happen when controversy erupted:

In the old days they sent down Naomi Gurian. At that time, Naomi was an assistant, she wasn't director of the Guild, and Naomi would usually sit in with the minority committees, *always* in the Black Writers Committee. And as a matter of fact, one time I was dealing with a lawyer and I had tried to bring this lawyer in to investigate, to take some statistics and Naomi came running down the hall, like with a knife, making a joke about, "get out! get out of here!" Their strategy was "Just keep the lid on them. If you hear them starting anything, stop it fast!"

Another black writer claimed that the Guild would simply rechannel complaints and not act upon them. "You go to the Guild every day with discrimination and they say, 'Well, it has to go to our legal department,' and they go round and round and nothing happens—ever."

Most minority writers agreed that the Guild has not effectively dealt with their particular problems. Despite minority participation on Guild-supervised committees, a time-consuming effort, none of these writers reported the successful resolution of any problem. At best, the Guild facilitated interaction between producers or studio representatives and minority writers. And here the outcome was rarely satisfactory. In one instance, the Guild arranged a meeting between a major production company and the African-American writers accusing them of racial discrimination. The meeting was short-circuited when it was announced that two of the black writers scheduled to participate had been hired by the company.

The Guild's role as a bargaining unit went unmentioned. Instead, discussion centered on the Guild's failure to address minority needs. One writer detailed the struggle to install an elevator for disabled individuals simply to ensure physical access to the Writers Guild building. Under the threat of picketing and a law suit, the Guild board was finally moved to action. However, in order to install the elevator, the Guild must acquire a larger parking lot, according to municipal building code, stalling further action. Clearly, the concerns of groups differ and minority activism within the Guild is often uncoordinated and confused.

There may be some validity to the minority claims. Overall, minorities felt underrepresented in Guild operations. This perception reinforced minority writers' sense of distance from Hollywood. Within the Guild, they form an alternative Guild, heading their own organizations, committees, and network of contacts. The writers are separate, possibly not equal, and left to battle among themselves. One writer cracked that the Human Resources Coordinating Committee (HRCC) has "seventeen members and eight factions." Another described meetings filled with the rancor of writers arguing over the importance of race vs. sex discrimination. At one meeting an African-American man declared that women writers were neither a minority nor serious professionals, insisting they worked in Hollywood while looking for producer-husbands. This somewhat militant individual did not reappear at any meetings after his outburst. Aside from the dramatics, the HRCC meetings failed to generate productive strategies or objectives. Chronically one person short of a quorum, they can rarely organize a vote.

The Writers Guild relationship to minority writers is troubled, its future role in minority action is unclear. Although the Guild claims its efforts are sincere, its overall effectiveness is dubious. Minority writers were forced to seek other means of satisfaction. Several discussed the importance of combining forces.

These writers developed the idea that the differing minorities would have to recognize their commonly held interests. "The mood is changing now in Hollywood, where there are a lot of people who have been left out and frustrated for a long time and they are pretty organized," one African-American woman explained. "But this is something that's gone on in the past: all the groups are out there separated and...scrambling over this very small piece of the pie and in ways we are working against each other. Now, we've got too many people who are considered minorities in the Writers Guild who don't see they all have something in common, the majority won't let them in. And we all need to work together on that problem."

Recognizing the dilemma of minorities fighting each other instead of the actual problem, another disabled writer remarked that "lately we have had meetings together where there have been Hispanics and the disabled committee and women and blacks and there are problems that we have that are very similar, some are very different and there is nothing you can do about that that, but as long as we start thinking that we are not enemies, there will be change. The enemy is out there. We cannot fight among each other—we'll never get anything done. Everyone is worried about being politically correct. I think we should worry less about using the right labels and more about changing the structure."

The Alternative Elite

One way in which minority writers resembled one another was in the creation of an "alternative elite" from their ranks. This alternative elite was composed of individuals who were viewed as "heroes" or "role models" and included publicly recognized figures as well as unrecognized but successful minority writers. Members of differing "protected classes" named the same figures and many were both proud and protective of this alternative elite.

One of the individuals most frequently mentioned was Bill Cosby. He was repeatedly identified as an unqualified success, lauded as the creator of a television situation comedy that did not stereotype African-Americans. One black writer explained that he liked the Cosby show because "it let white America know that there are black people who do live just like they do, that there are black people who have the same concerns." Several writers commented that the Cosby show's popular success had not depended on portraying blacks as jive-talking ghetto dwellers, finding humor in their poverty. Instead, Cosby depicted his television family as individuals, not blacks. "I think it's great, I loved it," one writer recalled. "One of the problems that I see as a black person, is that people think of you as being black before they think of you as being a person. I liked that show because it was really not about black people, although they were black. *Cosby* was not popular because the family was black, I think it was popular because it was just a show that really everybody could relate to."

Many minority writers were pleased that Cosby's character, Clifford Huxtable, was a doctor, that he and his family lived as upscale professionals and that the show was not based on exploring the comedic aspects of racial and ethnic differences. A Latino writer explained, that "Cosby came along with a wonderful idea that cut across all kinds of ethnic lines and was a show that, just like *Roots*, everybody could relate to. Cosby does a warm, wonderful family drama—we've all grown up in families—regardless of the color of the people in that show, we all related to the experience of being in a family."

Aside from his creativity, Cosby was also admired as an emerging power in Hollywood. One writer went so far as to identify him as the only possible candidate to become the first African-American network head. Many minority writers were heartened by the rumors he was attempting to purchase NBC. Not surprisingly, despite Cosby's ability to wield power he was vulnerable to criticism. Several writers recounted stories portraying him as extremely tyrannical. One black female writer praised certain aspects of the Cosby show but also expressed some concerns:

He does it so well. I am sure there are drawbacks with even Bill Cosby having as much power as he does, but he still does it so well. There might have been stories cause I've heard rumors, "rumors from the east," that he tampered with the scripts a lot and there were certain episodes that I watched in the last year where I thought there had been some tampering. During the last season I think I loved every episode that was on every show. It was just a slice of life, it didn't have to have a big story but it was so real and it was something that everyone could identify with. And there were some things that year that I thought were kind of glitzy, getting certain stars in there. I think he has to be careful not to get carried away with his own fame. Look what happened with that show he tried to do—*You Bet Your Life*—it proved he's not perfect, he's not God. But he was and is a brilliant entertainer.

Several writers also criticized Cosby for failing to hire minority, particularly black, writers. "Cosby had a wonderful show," one writer began. "It was a great thing but as far as making work and creating jobs for minorities, it didn't do that. They had to embarrass them [into] putting a black writer on the show, take an ad in the black papers, *seriously*, they had to do this to get a black writer on the show. God, if it was that difficult with a show like Cosby, imagine how difficult it is for everyone else."

Another writer remarked, "I think at one point they didn't even have one black staff writer on the Cosby show and that was a problem. It tells you that a lot of people have reason not to be optimistic."

One black writer revealed his experience trying to work for Cosby:

When they first got ready to do that show, they contacted me and asked me for two scripts to send them. I sent them two scripts and they said, "We like your stuff and we're gonna do the show in New York." I knew at the same time they contacted a number of white writers, they offered to fly them out to New York, find them accommodations and guaranteed them anywhere from six weeks staff work to five complete shows, all right? And the black writers they contacted, they said, "You can come out on spec, we will talk to you about a script, we're not paying any plane fares, we're not paying any accommodations." This writer proceeded to express his disappointment at the unexpected discrimination practiced by the Cosby organization.

Almost every minority writer remarked on Cosby's success and power. However, African-American writers, both male and female, elaborated to the greatest extent. They were the most invested and the most critical of Cosby, mentioning his tendency to overemploy white writers and staff. In general, however, he was valued as a model of minority success in Hollywood without sacrifice of minority identity. One writer explained why Cosby was a hero: "That show was passed on by ABC. People didn't think that it was going to work. They only saw it as a black family show. Cosby insisted this was a show about a wonderful family with warm relationships. A big part of his struggle was getting someone, a network to follow through. That's how he broke new ground." Another writer described his excitement over the rumored prospect of Cosby purchasing a major network. "That is what we want," she explained, "Not to be sitting in the back room any more but to be one of the players. Can you imagine a brother owning a network? I think, only then, could whites learn about power and oppression, all the problems they are so quick to identify and slow to change."

The alternative elite was not composed exclusively of black males, however. Several women were also identified as part of this select group. Winnifred Hervey, the writer-producer of the successful television sitcom *The Golden Girls* was described as "*the* black female success story." Women writers also named Clinton intimate Linda Bloodworth-Thomason and Suzanne de Passe of *Lonesome Dove* fame as examples of women enjoying creative and financial power. Roseanne Arnold was also signified as a role model, one woman commenting on the power she exerted, "She forced her husband on the networks, she virtually controls ABC and Roseanne isn't anyone's victim. It's refreshing."

Women selected both male and female role models but no male minority writer included a woman in his alternative elite. After rhapsodizing about the multiple abilities of Spike Lee (e.g., writer, director, editor), one black male writer thought of another talented individual who also "does everything," but in describing this woman, he could not remember her name.

Ironically, most members of the alternative elite were African-American, even those named by other minority groups. Aside from the few individuals all minorities agreed upon, writers designated different heroes. Statuses of writers and their chosen models appeared related: less successful writers named lower-status role models. Still, there were certain individuals who transcended categories and were admired by all minority writers, regardless of their sex, age, status, or ethnicity.

Although Cosby was touted by many African-American writers as a role model, the individual of the hour was clearly Spike Lee. There was a wide range of reactions to him, but virtually every writer of color commented on Spike Lee and most writers surveyed viewed him as a positive role model. Several African-American writers worried that Lee has alienated the Hollywood establishment. Their concern, they admitted, ran primarily to self-interest.

I think what he says and does is great but I keep wondering how it's gonna get me in the end. I mean, he's a talented guy but no one mainstream wants to touch him—look at what happened with the Academy Awards nominations. And I'm afraid that someday, someone is gonna look at me and—pardon the expression—tar me with the same brush—they'll see another African-American man with talent who is gonna make trouble and I'll be out of work. Or they'll buy my screenplay but I won't get to direct. It's okay that no one wants to back Spike Lee—he's got a track record, he can find outside money, but what about the rest of us?

Other writers differed, many insisting, "Cosby talks a lot but he gets in bed with the suits. Spike delivers—he takes on the suits and wins." His alleged anti-Semitism was also discussed: "I think what bothers white Hollywood is that Spike has made some supposedly anti-Semitic statements. I don't know if it's true—I do know the media distorts things to sell a story. I think that's why everybody is so scared. But I don't think a guy like Spike Lee is necessarily anti-Semitic, he's opinionated but he's not a bigot." Overall, feelings of admiration for Lee were discussed. He was labeled a "visionary," an "artist," and a "righteous brother, he hasn't forgotten where he came from." Most importantly, he was viewed as someone who extended opportunities to other writers, helping them, hiring them, and acting as a role model for other minorities. "One thing that's great about Spike—from the gaffer to the ADA to the line producer—everyone on the crew is African-American or a person of color. I know it's sort of reverse discrimination but I love it. Finally, we're in control." Interestingly, many Latino writers also expressed great admiration for Spike Lee, stating they wished such a Latino auteur would rise from their ranks to claim similar status. "I thought Luis Valdez would do it, but there's been no real breakthrough.

There's also this guy—Neal Jimenez—who wrote and directed the *Waterdance* although he doesn't identify himself as a Latino. I can't think of one figure I use as a role model." Another writer stated it more directly: "No Latino male has emerged as 'in your face' as Spike." Instead, the name many Latinos invoked in their alternative elite belonged not to a writer but to an actor who has also directed films and attracted attention during the Los Angeles rebellion following the initial Rodney King trial verdict. "The man for Latinos today is Edward James Olmos," one writer informed me. When pressed that he was not a writer she continued, "He may not be strictly a writer but he is an artist, he does more than act—did you see that movie he directed, *American Me*? He represents the values of our world, of our culture, he articulates them for us. I feel proud that he represents a Latino view in the mainstream. And he is popular with a cross section of America." Olmos was cast as a genuine culture-maker, working to transmit values to both Anglo and Latino communities.

Gay writers who were interviewed expressed their concern that so many potential role models were "in the closet," or "quietly gay," or "so silent they need to be outed." Many claimed that influential and powerful members of the entertainment industry were less likely to come out as they gained more power. "The best moment I had in my search for a role model," one writer explained,

was the night David Geffen officially came out himself. He'd always hedged his bets with this bullshit that he was bisexual because—what was it he said?—you had a better chance on Saturday night. I was angry, for years, that he tried to stay out of the politics or the process but I think now, yeah, someone like David comes out and more people in the velvet mafia might come clean. I mean, come on, look at someone like Barry Diller who's been quietly gay all these years. Or Jodie Foster—don't sue me for saying that, I don't know if Jodie wants to be outed.

Another writer explained,

Either you come out right away, you say I'm a gay writer, that's it, or I'm a writer who happens to be gay and that's it or you don't come out until you're as powerful as, say, David Geffen and no one can hurt you or you come out if the *Enquirer* runs your picture saying you're HIV-positive. Even then I know people in the industry who would rather have people believe they're IV-drug abusers who got the virus. They're saying I'd rather be known as a junkie than a gay male. Shit, what kind of a role model is that?

Still, many writers emphasized the importance of belonging to the network of gay writers in Hollywood. Instead of concentrating on an alternative elite, several gay writers expressed satisfaction with personal contacts that had proved meaningful in their careers. As one woman explained, "Who needs a role model? I know someone who'll take my calls."

Certain writers were rejected by minority writers and not considered part of any alternative elite. Richard Pryor was most frequently criticized for having abused and destroyed the optimal opportunities available to him. One writer detailed the difficulties he encountered with Pryor's company, Indigo Productions. "He never works," another writer revealed. "As an African-American, there's an embarrassment that I feel there. Although I understand he's very ill, so that may explain some of the problems of the past." Pryor was also criticized for overestimating his abilities. "I think he's a uniquely talented individual," one writer remarked, "but actors should act, producers should produce, studio heads should run studios and I don't think Richard's a filmmaker, it's not his strong suit. He's an actor and a comedian."

Minority writers also felt they could not identify Eddie Murphy in their alternative elite, although for different reasons. As one of the leading actors at the box office in the United States and internationally, he is acknowledged as commanding power and attention. Nonetheless, several writers expressed dismay that Murphy had not used his position to forward the status of people of color in Hollywood. One complained that instead of using minority writers, "Eddie's got Neil Simon and other white writers waiting in line." Their rejection of Murphy, among others, demonstrated that minority writers made choices in identifying a power elite.

Their alternative elite offered examples of what minorities could achieve in Hollywood, despite obstacles and discrimination. Such an elite also served deeper psychological needs. Individuals were praised for not surrendering their identities to "the system." Using successful individuals as role models enabled minority writers to integrate their conflicting identities as minorities and as writers. Whatever the actual impact of an alternative elite, the idealization of such individuals alleviated minority frustration.

Outside Intervention

Building from their alternative elite, minority writers discussed resources for political change that existed outside the structure of the Hollywood establishment. As part of the political solutions sought by Hollywood's minorities, outside intervention was often mentioned as a possibility. One African-American woman writer stated:

If we are not able to do it, I think we are going to start bringing outside pressure on them. I am not one that would normally look to a group like the NAACP to come in and change Hollywood, because I think a lot of the people that work at the NAACP don't understand the way Hollywood works and a lot of times what they do is more harmful than good but over the next few years, if you still find yourself really frustrated, you're gonna have to get more creative about what you are going to be able to do. I think a lot of people are at the point where they are not just gonna sit back and say nothing because they've got nothing else to lose.

Many minority writers discounted the efforts of the NAACP. Although mentioned frequently, the organization was characterized as anachronistic and ineffectual. One writer recalled the NAACP's abortive efforts to investigate discrimination in Hollywood:

I can remember three years ago a guy from the NAACP national office came out here and he wanted to—they were talking about a boycott at the time. So we met with him, me and a couple of other people met with him. We said, "We'll, meet with you and we want to be sure that when you go in and have a meeting with those guys [studio executives, network executives] that you'll ask the right questions." I must have spent four or five hours, about every night a week, and he had a stenographer there, a paid stenographer, just taking it down and he didn't learn a thing, he didn't do a thing. There was a rumor that some guys at one of the studios bought his ass outta there before he found out too much.

In all, the NAACP was viewed as highly visible but impotent. Their 1986 media outcry over the motion picture *The Color Purple* was viewed as a public relations fiasco. One black female writer laughed that the NAACP criticized the film for its portrayal of black males and then criticized the Academy of Motion Picture Arts and Sciences for failing to honor the film with any major academy awards. "How could you be angry that a film you felt was negative hadn't won any awards? Wouldn't you feel vindicated?" she asked.

Recently, the value of the NAACP has been reconsidered. Several writers felt their pro-active, positive stance towards changing Hollywood may actually work. "Instead of going on protests," one woman analyzed, "they seem to be working more *with* the establishment. Some people might think of it as selling out but I think it's the way to win big time."

Still, minority writers expressed optimism over other possibilities. Several mentioned legal action as another untried step that might be taken to resolve the inequities minorities encountered in Hollywood. One African-American writer compared the effectiveness of the judicial system with the much blighted NAACP when asked how much longer Hollywood's white establishment could continue to say "no" to minority talent, remarking, "They can keep saying no forever and ever until people challenge them, until legally if the courts or somebody says, 'Hey enough already, honey.' There have been attempts at it and threats and the local NAACP which is a joke but no one's really tried the courts and they've got to."

The feasibility of legal action was raised by another writer who stated, "We should not be talking about the morality of the situation, nor the good the American public would receive. Instead we should talk about what effect not hiring minorities would have on the business, how we're going to court as soon as possible. How we're going to do anything. It has to be something that directly affects the business."

Inherent in this last statement is an important guide to political action not always appreciated by minority writers. The "business of Hollywood" has not been affected by minority anger or activism. Until industry operations and earnings are affected, change may not be achieved. One minority writer summarized the situation:

You have to wrap it [activism] with the business in some way and I am not certain of that way yet. I think it might be the courts. I think the community-action legal firms in the area might be the way that this is finally achieved, because I don't think it's going to be achieved by the industry. It's just, they've had years and years and years and nothing really happens. They find someone and he works out well. Instead of them saying, "Well, boy, this is okay, let's open the doors," they just say, "here's a fluke," or they use that just as an example of how far they have come and so on and they don't use it as a way of saying, "it works, let's now open the doors, let's make sure they stay open" and the people who are in charge of hiring are never given the mandate that you must hire...or we're going to take away your ability to produce shows and the only people who can do that are studios and networks and that's the situation.

Many minority writers, particularly African-Americans, named Jesse Jackson as potential agent of change. One explained that it was "Jesse Jackson and Operation PUSH boycotting CBS and the CBS station in Chicago—that got some changes. They got them...that's the kind of group that could do us some good." Jackson was praised as a successful politician who is, according to minorities at least, beyond reproach. Given the anti-Semitism many minority writers express, Jackson may be a sympathetic figure for other reasons. Along with Jackson, several writers mentioned Louis Farrakhan as another important instigator of change although he was seen as "more volatile" and "less mainstream" than Jackson.

While outside resources were considered, government intervention was ruled out as a possibility by most minorities. "Politics is the movie business all over," one writer claimed. "Most studios have a guy who is friendly with the Democratic Party, one for the Republicans, so no matter who gets elected, no one gets pissed on."

One African-American writer specified the type of individual or group needed to effect change in Hollywood:

It's like Caesar's wife, somebody has gotta be above reproach, y'know? So it's got to be a group that's not looking to curry favor, that's not looking for something...in this industry there is an expression, it's a crudity, that we use, everybody's a starfucker, y'know what I mean? Everybody gets into the glamour of Hollywood and they want to be, they want to become producers. Of course. So it's got to be somebody or some group who is not a starfucker, who cannot be seduced...I can't do it because of the fact that I am making my livelihood out there...and these people buy people off! They dangle the gold they carry...Everybody's got round heels.

Politics and Creativity

Many writers who were politically involved have not been professionally successful. The same people who provided an excellent fund of political information grew silent when asked to discuss creative processes and professional output. Remaining involved with minority causes while developing artistically in the Hollywood community presented a dilemma for many. Indeed, minority writers were not torn between art and commerce so much as art and activism. A black female commented, "After political involvement, you have to start thinking, what am I doing artistically?" Another writer discussed how political activities have affected his productivity:

I should have made five or six films by now, but I haven't because of the reality of what's going on...it's really the situation, it's because there is a struggle that is taking place to make a better industry and if some people, a few people working inside and there are people working outside and if you recognize that it's a struggle and you want to be part of it, then you have to accept that you will be less productive.

When asked what would enable him to give up his political activities and devote himself to writing, the writer flatly said, "It would take a change in the whole society, that's what it would take."

The actual impact of outside minority activism upon the industry is unclear. Certainly, minority writers have drawn attention to their situation and lack of status in Hollywood. With the emergence of newer, more powerful political alliances and outside intervention, greater change may be engendered. Still, in a reasoned approach to the problem, one writer suggested a blending of artistic and political concerns:

I am writing...a wonderful, wonderful script, collaborating with someone which I haven't done in a long, long time and this script is capable of doing as much if not perhaps even more than a political action right this instant because all art is political if it's any good. All art is political. So what you have to do is you have to recognize that there really is no division between the two activities and you just have to make sure that you are not trying to do it all by yourself.

The Future

In discussing the future of minority writers, there was a wide range of opinion. One-half of the minority writers expressed ambivalence or were ambivalent to positive outlooks. The remaining half were extremely negative, often marshaling information to support their claims. One black writer cited numerous examples:

When you think that CBS Television, in its entertainment division, does not have one single black executive. They are always using the excuse "the cutbacks, the cutbacks." That's why Operation PUSH boycotted them...they don't have one single black person. ABC the *American* Broadcasting Company, has one little black woman, and they are trying to get rid of her, at a very low level. NBC has more than anybody but there's no black executives controlling Prime Time Television. The Fox network has no one...and one of their hottest shows is *In Living Color*!

Another writer was extremely pessimistic that minorities would ever exert any substantive control in Hollywood, remarking, "There will never be an African-American studio head, at least, not in our time. I am older than you and not even in your time, because you are going to live longer than me...the only way it will ever happen is if you get somebody who has so much clout, let's say a Bill Cosby. Say Cosby had five shows on the air and this and that and he said, 'Okay, I'm gonna run a studio,' maybe, maybe...Eddie Murphy, maybe. But you know, again, I doubt it."

A Latino woman remarked, "Based on what I think about a person, I may say, 'I think she or he has what it takes,' but as far as collectively, as a group—Latinos—or as a group—blacks—I am not very optimistic about their future."

Another minority writer bleakly predicted, "It's going to get worse and I'll tell you why. Money. Power. That's why. We've been figureheads, as people of color. We've never really had money or power and it's getting harder to come by, not easier."

Negative responses predominated among individuals who had achieved little to moderate success in Hollywood. However, minority attitudes towards the future were not exclusively a function of success. Several relatively unsuccessful minority writers remained extremely positive about the future.

A few writers equivocated when asked their predictions, characterizing conditions neither as improving nor worsening. "Well, it cannot get any worse, I mean, come on," one writer scoffed, "One hundred and some minority writers in the Writers Guild out of 7000...I mean, it cannot possibly get any worse, I think." He was joined by other writers who were equally vague, often digressing to other subjects.

Several writers remained convinced that the minority future in Hollywood was bright. Women writers were especially positive. "Things are happening now," one woman insisted, "that I could not have imagined even five years ago. I certainly believe that anyone—any woman, African-American, Latino—any minority who is talented and has good ideas will succeed, will see their work produced." Another woman observed that "Callie Khouri won the Academy Award and Hillary got in the White House—I feel like anything is possible!"

Other minority writers were more guarded in their expectations. One African-American writer explained that although things were improving, the situation remained disturbing:

See when now we're 1.6% of the industry and if in 1974 it was half that...I guess you could say, if you wanted to say things in a favorable manner, you'd say black participation in the Guild has doubled in the last 20 years...the statistics are misleading because there aren't any actual numbers here...There is always progress but by the time we have become properly represented in the Guild, there may no longer be a Guild as we know it. They will be off doing other things. Maybe robots will be doing all the writing by the time we are properly represented. So something should be done now, if it's ever going to be done.

Opinion varied widely concerning the future of minorities in Hollywood. Writers offered evidence to support their positions. Anecdotes were recounted and statistics cited, but the future remains uncertain. One black female writer coupled a positive outlook with a suggestion for improving status:

It's staying power and that's the key. There are a lot of minority writers who have come and gone and they never do anything again and that's not helping us at all. If you have some minority writers and they have staying power that will help change things over time—because then they can bring in more people. It's going to be hard for them and they shouldn't have the pressure of having to solve the minority problem when they've got a job to do. But if you can get some people in there with staying power and who can show certain whites who have it in their minds that people just can't do it; to be a writer you've got to be short and Jewish, they make jokes about it all the time but they really mean it...so do I see it changing? Yes, but slowly, very slowly. And with a lot of work.

Notes

[1]Information on individuals' disabilities was not available from Guild files so the study did not include statistics on disabled writers.

[2]It was decided that most writers over 40 had previous experience in Hollywood, making them ineligible for the script submission program.

Chapter Eight

Conclusion

All of these writers talked extensively about what it was like to work in the entertainment industry. As a result, a more complete picture of Hollywood writers emerged, which involved their identities and their relationships to the industry. Hollywood writers did not split on every issue and the dichotomy between minority and majority was a concept that did not always reflect reality. In many cases, majority and minority responses overlapped and—at times—were identical. These shared perceptions suggest that their identities as writers occasionally transcended minority or majority status.

Shared Perceptions
All writers shared certain qualities. As a group, they rarely critiqued their own writing or discussed their creative abilities. Writers avoided any serious discussion of their talents, often using humor or making jokes to avoid the subject altogether. Their brief comments on their abilities were indirect and usually positive. Writers described awards they received and screenplays sold, but few mentioned writing problems they had endured. There was no self-criticism, no mention of writer's block, creative difficulty, or professional failure. Despite the fact these writers willingly discussed personal intimacies, they all shied away from the issue of talent.

What was openly discussed, described, and complained about by every writer interviewed was the unavailability and unpredictability of employment. Majority and minority responses were identical. Despite differing perceptions of access, all writers felt that opportunities were limited and hiring practices inconsistent. Many pointed out that with a Writers Guild membership numbering 6000 plus, competition for the 500 to 600 yearly feature film and television projects remained fierce. Three thousand of these 6000 members have joined in the past ten years and as the Guild grows, the proportion of jobs to members also decreases. Some writers insisted that, currently, fewer writers work than ever before, claiming producers played favorites and offered particular writers multiple projects. Along with the limited opportunities and inconsistent hiring practices, writers declared it was impossible to predict whether an idea or a script would sell.

Many writers also touched on the problem of "previous experience." They explained that it was almost impossible to obtain assignments or sell scripts without "previous experience." However, it was equally impossible to obtain experience without being offered the opportunity to work. Writers lamented that networks, studios, and production companies constantly rejected projects they would have accepted from other writers with the requisite experience or background.

Still, previous experience did not guarantee professional security. Even individuals who had held studio staff positions or sold screenplays for six figures complained that one's status as a writer involved constant uncertainty. Several writers remembered Sunday night, eleventh-hour firings suffered by first-time contract novices and award-winning veterans alike. One writer was proud about working on one studio lot for an entire year, a record of longevity several writers agreed was remarkable. Still, when questioned, none of these writers indicated they were seriously considering abandoning screenwriting due to employment uncertainties.

Their commitment to screenwriting also emerged in writers' remarks on the division between creative and financial considerations, the dichotomy viewed as "art vs. money." Financial concerns were not discussed in any detail by either group. Initially, majority writers issued a "disclaimer," insisting they wrote for Hollywood only to make money. However, it became apparent that other motives influenced their efforts and money was rarely mentioned following the disclaimer. Minority writers expressed even less involvement with financial gain. This is not to assert that writers denied financial necessity as well as material indulgence. All writers discussed the allure of the "good life" and their desire to enjoy security and privilege. Nonetheless, the desire to earn money did not dominate their creative efforts. Most claimed the "art vs. money" dichotomy posed in interviews was meaningless. Instead, Hollywood writers described other motives driving their work involving personal issues of identity and cultural concerns. Their writing clearly served personal needs, different from those conventionally anticipated.

Varied Perceptions

Both majority and minority writers agreed on certain problems they faced in Hollywood. But even though the *same* problem was described by each group, their emphases and concerns differed.

A key issue discussed by both majority and minority writers was control. Due to their preoccupation with access, several minority writers only touched on the issue briefly. But the minority writers who had achieved success in Hollywood discussed their feelings of powerlessness in depth. In struggling for creative control, minority and majority writers faced the same obstacles: demanding "stars," authoritarian directors, fiscally oriented producers, and the interference of the system. However, when discussing their problems with control, minority writers often added in their concerns over discrimination in the industry.

While minority discussions frequently returned to the subject of discrimination, majority writers focused on creative control. For many, success was limited and employment inconsistent but despite their tenuous positions, majority writers remained focused on the fate of their writing. Any positive aspects of a script were due to their talent, any faults were due to outside tampering. Majority writers consistently complained that scripts were "ruined" by other principals in the entertainment industry. Indulging feelings of possessiveness, they voiced dismay at what happened to their work when subjected to the machinations of Hollywood production. Several had worked or planned to work in positions as producers or directors, claiming these positions afforded them more control over their work. If they had not had any role in the final production, majority writers downplayed their role in its final outcome.

Writers' relationships with the entertainment industry were cast in terms of control. Their relationship to American culture was not as clear. In explaining how they perceived American mass culture and its interaction with their work, writers made confused and contradictory statements. Both majority and minority writers discussed their potential roles as culture-makers. However, their willingness to accept such responsibility differed markedly.

While majority writers acknowledged their membership in the Hollywood elite, they were reluctant to label themselves culture-makers. When the idea was raised, their immediate reaction was dismissal. They underplayed their role or spoke vaguely about the relationship between the media and society. However, as discussion continued, several majority writers described how they "made" culture; how they wished, *in certain instances*, to transmit ideas, values, messages—no matter how subtle—within their scripts. Majority writers perceived themselves as separate from and acting upon American culture. They sought to characterize themselves as rising above both Hollywood *and* mass culture. Majority writers denied American culture's impact upon them and made little mention of how American culture affected their lives or their work.

Minority writers identified themselves as "culture-makers" much more readily. In addition, they emphasized Hollywood's impact on American culture to a greater degree than majority writers. Rather than reluctantly acknowledging their roles in making culture, they claimed the status enthusiastically. All minority writers described efforts to insert messages or transmit values in their writing. They emphasized the importance of their educating and enlightening the public.

However, in emphasizing their roles as culture-makers, minority writers may ignore the needs of the audience. The personal experiences they bring to their writing, the reasons why they write, and their preoccupation with being accepted in Hollywood may militate against this. While minority writers lamented their inability to sell "stories that should be told," majority writers focused on creating empathy between their work and audiences. It is unclear whether minority writers write scripts as marketable as those written by their white male counterparts. Several minority writers conceptualized audiences as passive recipients of material they wished to present, others did not discuss audiences at all. Successful majority and minority writers discussed potential "viewers" more extensively.

Majority writers expressed varying regard for their perceived audiences. At times, they were condescending, insisting the American public desired a steady diet of sex and violence, at least on their television and movie screens. However, majority writers also credited audiences with exercising discretion and independence in terms of choice and preference. The public was viewed as an active, if inconsistent, force that writers had to consider.

Those writers who were adamant about what their writing would and should achieve were less successful than the individuals who did not present the manufacture of culture as a primary concern. Ultimately, successful Hollywood writers were culture-makers by default. They arrived at this role unintentionally. Using their own experience and ability to communicate, they reached their audiences and influenced them in ways of which they remained unaware.

Differences Between Majority and Minority Writers

The key differences between minority and majority writers revolved around identity issues rather than the politics of Hollywood. The difference in majority and minority writers' identities showed up most strongly in their inner vs. outer orientations.[1] Majority writers were strongly inner-directed. The issues they discussed concerned creativity, working out personal conflicts through writing, and maintaining some semblance of control over their work. Minority writers, on the other hand, were outer-directed. They focused on their relationship to Hollywood and their attempts as individuals and groups to gain access and ultimately transform its structure.

Many successful minority writers were faced with bridging these orientations. Although they remained partly outer-directed, continuing efforts to modify the attitudes and discrimination in Hollywood, they also expressed concerns over their writing and creative control. The minority writers who did not experience this dynamic were individuals who did not identify with their minority status, denying its importance in their lives as writers.

Majority writers discussed ideas and creativity extensively, explaining how personal experience surfaced in their scripts. Because of their psychological investment, majority writers were preoccupied with controlling production of their work. But while majority writers desired control over their own scripts, minority writers demanded a voice in the content of programs with which they had nothing to do. Many railed at the Hollywood establishment for portraying minorities stereotypically. Responsibility was projected and minority problems were attributed to external sources.

Many minority writers blamed their blocked entry to Hollywood on discrimination and the failure of industry powers to recognize minority ability. In clinging to their minority identities, these writers failed to align themselves with the Hollywood majority, often resorting to hostility and couching their observations in extreme anti-Semitic sentiment. Their inability to identify with the industry establishment meant that minority writers served, in part, as architects of their own exclusion. Beyond that, lacking an inner-directedness, minority writers often did not entertain or admit any personal responsibility for their problems. The difference in focus and perspective was marked and affected the fate of each group in Hollywood.

Most importantly, there was a marked division in how majority and minority writers "made sense" of Hollywood. Successful minority writers possessed an excellent understanding of the industry. But the majority writers, irrespective of success, all exhibited a keen Hollywood "sense." They described industry operations, often more knowingly than minorities, establishing themselves as "insiders." This appeared to be a mutually reinforcing phenomenon. Most majority writers were Jewish, sharing language, rituals, and culture with many of the powerful in Hollywood. A few minority writers demonstrated their understanding of this reality, even including Yiddish phrases in their remarks. However, their knowledge was secondhand and for them, "insider" status was not as easily acquired.

Several minority and majority writers agreed, minorities did not adequately understand the customs of Hollywood. They were not well versed in the rules of social interaction. Not having access to the industry, lacking knowledge of a shared cultural tradition and, in some cases, their own hostility, all restricted minority writers in developing a Hollywood sense. Instead, they created stereotypes of their own. They viewed Hollywood powers as perpetually driving Mercedes, living on the west side of Los Angeles and ignoring reality. This further inhibited their understanding the entertainment industry.

Majority writers, some less successful than some minorities, all exhibited an enhanced working knowledge of Hollywood. These individuals' Hollywood sense reinforced their internal orientation. Their understanding and acceptance of the industry infrastructure freed them from preoccupation with Hollywood. Minority writers, often unsuccessful or inconsistently successful at gaining access, devoted energy to comprehending the underpinnings of the industry. Their effort, in turn, reinforced their external orientation.

Another difference supported the fundamental division in orientation. These writers varied in their political activism and involvement in the Writers Guild. Majority writers were completely divorced from Writers Guild activities. They viewed their membership in the Guild with detachment, it made no difference in their status and functioning as writers. Majority writers perceived the Guild as weak, ineffectual, and completely beside the point. But minority writers acted in complete contrast. With two exceptions, minority writers were, or had been, extremely involved with the Writers Guild. They had organized action groups and served on Guild committees, often as chairpersons. Minority political commitment was total and involvement with the Guild was strong. This is not to say the Guild escaped criticism. Several minority writers expressed extreme rage and frustration at its inertia. Still, the minority writers generally felt they needed the Guild as a vehicle for advance. Many appeared to rely on an outside structure or organization to forward their aims, uncertain that their individual abilities would insure success in Hollywood. In contrast, majority writers maintained that their own abilities and luck determined their success or failure. Beyond calling strikes and setting pay scales, majority individuals felt there was little the Writers Guild or any outside organization could do; they were responsible for themselves.

Their outer-directedness was also apparent when minority writers described writing topics they considered objectionable. All minority writers wanted to avoid scripts involving stereotypical or negative depictions of minority groups. Many writers elaborated that they could write a negative portrayal of one person of color or minority individual, but not an entire group. While not every objection concerned minorities, most minority responses were political in tone. Their remarks constantly considered the outside structure and general minority concerns.

The topics majority writers considered objectionable were consistent with their inner-directedness. Political concerns were not discussed. Instead, majority writers wished to avoid topics that conflicted with personal beliefs, rejecting screenplays that involved betrayal, evil, and injustice. In addition, they discussed their inability to develop characters with whom they could not identify.

Their internal orientation was particularly evident in majority writers' preoccupation with characters they created. Focusing on characters and making them "real" was a way in which these writers examined themselves. Many majority writers admitted script content was often disguised personal experience, with characters representing certain facets of the writer's personality. Majority writers worked identity issues through in their writing. It was an extremely individual and personal process, free of concern with the industry or American culture. Not all writing was personally fulfilling. In some instances majority writers explained they simply completed assignments. Nonetheless, every majority writer described working through individual issues and personalizing the creative process. Respondents maintained that these experiences made the writing process worthwhile. Very few minority writers described a similar practice/experience.

Instead, minority writers concentrated on external concerns. Their writing efforts were played out against the backdrop of Hollywood and American culture. Several minority individuals appeared to be testing and revising their identities using the outside "white" world as a proving ground. In doing so they appeared inconsistent, uncommitted, and unreliable. On the one hand, almost every minority writer insisted that stereotyping be replaced with the fair, honest portrayal of minorities. Several minority writers clamored that they be allowed to tell their stories. However, while battling for fair portrayals, minority writers were equally insistent they not be viewed as minority "experts." They repeatedly stated that they wished to write scripts concerning something other than the experience of their particular minority group; specifically, scripts with majority, not minority, themes. Unfortunately, these demands contributed to minority writers' image of inconsistency, leaving them open to the charge that they lacked direction in their writing.

Minority writers' preoccupation with external concerns made their struggle more complicated. They blamed the structure, raged against it, longed for acceptance, and ultimately measured themselves against its standards. Unfortunately, this outer-directedness often prevented minorities from developing their own identities.

Identity

Each group of Hollywood writers worked out personal identity in a specific way. In general, majority writers dealt with intrapsychic concerns; they were more internally oriented. Their pursuits were individual; they focused on creativity, psychological conflicts, and control. Minority writers worked through identity issues with an external orientation. While focused on individual concerns, they maintained a more extensive involvement with outside structures. Beyond themselves, minorities concentrated on dealing with discrimination and fighting minority stereotypes in media portrayals. However, successful minority writers shared more characteristics with majority writers—including increased attention to intrapsychic and internal issues.

Both majority and minority individuals faced the problem of "belonging" to the Hollywood elite, without sacrificing identity. To a certain extent, successful majority writers established such a balance. For minority writers, however, the task was somewhat more complicated. They faced the dilemma of surrendering certain elements of their identities as minorities, maintaining others, and rationalizing the process to defend against accusations of betrayal and "selling out." They had to fit into the Hollywood establishment while maintaining personal integrity. The constant restructuring of individual identity constituted a complicated process for minority writers in Hollywood, exacerbated by their struggles for acceptance and concern over discrimination.

The minority writers who succeeded exhibited an openness in their identity and an ability to learn. They did not view the Hollywood establishment as their adversary. Instead, while they expressed concerns over their minority status, these writers accepted several premises: that talent is always valued, that effectively selling one's self is as important as having good material, and that it is necessary to possess some "sense" of Hollywood in order to succeed. In addition, most of these writers maintained their minority consciousness, explaining they did not feel any need to choose between the two.

The identity of "writer" exists apart from group concerns. Its orientation is more individual, the writer is internally rather than externally directed. Screenwriters frame their work in terms shared by all individuals. What is misleading about the "writer" identity is that while its focus is personal, it may reach a wide audience. This is the fundamental duality that majority writers have negotiated and minority writers, for the most part, are beginning to probe. It is difficult to accept the apparently contradictory notion that as an individual writer directs his/her focus more inward, s/he may create work with greater external appeal. For so long most minority writers have believed that the only way for them to succeed in Hollywood was to forward their own interests, reiterating their demand that minority stories *must* be told. Nonetheless, what is increasingly apparent is that the individuals who succeed as Hollywood writers possess the requisite writing talents to transform what occurs in their own lives into a story with general appeal—whatever its cultural content.

For these writers, work in Hollywood requires a tolerance for contradiction. Each must focus on individual concerns in a manner that will most effectively reach a large audience. They must possess some creative talent but also function as profiteers. The Hollywood writer should be a manipulator who can operate in a multi-billion-dollar enterprise with some knowledge of its workings, while maintaining personal integrity, even with so small a gesture as the naming of a character. Themes of control and surrender and identity vs. conformity dominated the lives of these individuals. But despite their own ambivalence and the dilemmas these individuals faced, they were committed to working as writers in Hollywood.

Notes

[1]Naturally, the dichotomy was not rigid. Most writers, regardless of status, mixed internal and external orientations. Minority writers were concerned with internal, intrapsychic issues in differing degrees just as majority writers were sensitive to the influence of external forces. However, overall minority responses indicated more consideration of the external, while majority writers were preoccupied with internal concerns.

Works Cited

Anger, Kenneth. *Hollywood Babylon*. New York: Simon and Schuster, 1975.

___. *Hollywood Babylon II*. New York: Dutton, 1983.

Bach, Steven. *Final Cut: Dreams and Disaster in the Making of Heaven's Gate*. New York: William Morrow, 1985.

Behlmer, Rudy. *Memo from David O. Selznick*. New York: Viking, 1972.

Berg, A. Scott. *Goldwyn: A Biography*. New York: Knopf, 1989.

Bergen, Candice. *Knock Wood*. New York: Ballantine, 1984.

Blumenthal, John. *The Official Hollywood Handbook*. New York: Simon and Schuster, 1984.

Bogdanovich, Peter. *Pieces of Time*. New York: Arbor House, 1973.

Brady, John. *The Craft of the Screenwriter: Interviews with Six Celebrated Screenwriters*. New York: Touchstone, 1981.

Bragg, Melvyn. *Richard Burton: A Life*. Boston: Little, Brown, 1989.

Brownstein, Ronald. *The Power and the Glitter*. New York: Pantheon, 1990.

Caine, Michael. *What's It All About?* New York: Random House, 1992.

Corliss, Richard. *Talking Pictures: Screenwriters in American Cinema*. Woodstock, NY: Overlook, 1974.

Didion, Joan. *After Henry*. New York: Simon and Schuster, 1992.

Dunne, John Gregory. *Quintana and Friends*. New York: Simon and Schuster, 1980.

___. *The Studio*. New York: Farrar, Straus and Giroux, 1969.

Dworkin, Susan. *Double DePalma*. New York: Newmarket, 1984.

___. *Making Tootsie*. New York: Newmarket, 1983.

Ebert, Roger. *A Kiss Is Still a Kiss*. New York: Andrews, McMeel and Parker, 1984.

Field, Syd. *Screenplay: The Foundations of Screenwriting*. New York: Delacorte, 1982.

Gabler, Neil. *An Empire of Their Own: How the Jews Invented Hollywood*. New York: Crown, 1988.

Glaser, Barney G., and Anselm M. Strauss. *The Discovery of Grounded Theory*. Chicago: Aldine, 1967.

Goldman, William. *Adventures in the Screen Trade*. New York: Warner, 1983.

___. *Hype and Glory*. New York: Villard, 1990.

155

Grant, Lee. "The Day of Decision for the Writers Guild." *Los Angeles Times* 10 Apr. 1981: VI.1.

Greenfeld, Josh. *The Return of Mr. Hollywood.* New York: Carroll and Graf, 1984.

Hamilton, Ian. *Writers in Hollywood.* New York: Harper and Row, 1990.

Haskell, Mollie. *From Reverence to Rape: The Treatment of Women in the Movies.* New York: Holt, Rinehart, and Winston, 1973.

Horn, John. "Gunfight at the Writers Guild Corral." *Los Angeles Times* 1 Sept. 1985, Calendar Sunday Supplement, 14.

Huston, John A. *An Open Book.* New York: Knopf, 1980.

Kael, Pauline. *Deeper Into Movies.* Boston: Atlantic Little-Brown, 1973.

___. *Going Steady.* Boston: Atlantic Little-Brown, 1970.

___. *I Lost It at the Movies.* Boston: Atlantic Little-Brown, 1965.

___. *Kiss Kiss Bang Bang.* Boston: Atlantic Little-Brown, 1968.

___. *Reeling.* Boston: Atlantic Little-Brown, 1976.

___. *Taking It All In.* New York: Holt, Rinehart, and Winston, 1984.

___. *When the Lights Go Down.* New York: Holt, Rinehart, and Winston, 1980.

Kelley, Kitty. *My Way: The Unauthorized Biography of Frank Sinatra.* New York: Bantam, 1986.

Lefcourt, Peter. *The Deal.* New York: Random House, 1991.

Litwak, Mark. *Reel Power: The Struggle for Influence and Success in the New Hollywood.* New York: Morrow, 1986.

MacGraw, Ali. *Moving Pictures.* New York: Bantam, 1991.

Maltin, Leonard. *The Whole Film Sourcebook.* New York: New American Library, 1983.

McClintick, David. *Indecent Exposure.* New York: Morrow, 1982.

McMurtry, Larry. *Film Flam.* New York: Simon and Schuster, 1987.

Medved, Michael. *Hollywood vs. America: Popular Culture and the War Against Traditional Values.* New York: Harper Collins, 1992.

Mordden, Ethan. *Movie Star: A Look at the Women Who Made Hollywood.* New York: St. Martin's, 1983.

O'Hara, John. *Hope of Heaven.* New York: Harcourt, Brace, 1938.

Powdermaker, Hortense. *Hollywood: The Dream Factory.* London: Secker and Warburg, 1950.

Ross, Lillian. *Picture.* New York: Proscenium, 1952.

Ross, Lillian, and Helen Ross. *The Player: A Profile of an Art.* New York: Proscenium, 1961.

Salomon, Julie. *The Devil's Candy.* Boston: Houghton Mifflin, 1991.

Schickel, Richard. *The Men Who Made the Movies*. New York: Atheneum, 1973.

Schulberg, Budd. *Moving Pictures: Memories of a Hollywood Prince*. New York: Stein and Day, 1981.

___. *What Makes Sammy Run?* New York: Random House, 1941.

Schwartz, Nancy Lynn. *The Hollywood Writers' Wars*. New York: Knopf, 1982.

Stein, Benjamin. *Hollywood Days, Hollywood Nights: The Diary of a Mad Screenwriter*. New York: Bantam, 1988.

Stuart, Linda. *Getting Your Script Through the Hollywood Maze*. Los Angeles: Acrobat, 1993.

Thomson, David. *Showman: The Life of David O. Selznick*. New York: Knopf, 1992.

___. "Trouble in Chinatown." *Vanity Fair* 48.11: 59-61, 125-29.

Tolkin, Michael. *The Player*. New York: Random House, 1989.

Viertel, Peter. *Dangerous Friends*. New York: Nan Talese, 1992.

___. *White Hunter, Black Heart*. New York: Dell, 1953.

Wagner, Bruce. *Force Majeure*. New York: Random House, 1991.

Wick, Steve. *Bad Company*. New York: Harcourt Brace Jovanovich, 1990.

Appendix

Interview Outline

1. Basic Demographic Information

   Age
   Education
   Ethnicity/race
   Marital status, family

2. Personal Background, Biographical

   Please give a brief biographical sketch of yourself, explaining how you became a Hollywood writer. Did you follow any particular career path? What were the greatest obstacles? Greatest supports?

3. Viewpoint

   After interviewing people in various aspects of entertainment production, I have a fairly good idea of the basic framework of the industry. I'd like to know more about writers.
   What do you think are the important issues to cover, questions to ask, of motion picture and television writers? (Or, what issues are important to writers?)

4. Identity

   How much of yourself do you see in your writing? How much do you draw upon personal experience in writing a screenplay? How much does your writing reflect your own thought?
   What are your priorities as a writer?
   Are there non-entertainment projects you are involved with (e.g., a novel)?

How do you deal with differing roles and different demands?
Are the influences different or similar in each type of writing you undertake?

5. Creativity and Talent

Could you discuss the actual process of writing? How do you do it? Could you discuss when and where you work? How your writing "unfolds"? Is there any set pattern you follow?

Describe your own creative process. What about talent? Discuss the importance of talent in your endeavor.

6 Control

As part of the process of creation/writing, how much control are you able to retain over your writing?

How do you feel about doing rewrites? What about someone else rewriting your work?

How important is creative control? How do you deal with its maintenance or its loss?

7. Art and Money

Are you aware of economic considerations and making money when you write? How does this affect you?

How much are you influenced by economic rewards vs. artistic fulfillment? (Is this a realistic dichotomy?)

Do you/would you ever want to produce something you had written?

8. Security

How much job "security" do you feel as a Hollywood writer?

Do you think you are more or less vulnerable than other individuals in the entertainment industry?

How would you respond to something like a blacklisting of writers that occurred during the McCarthy era?

Do you think writers are more protected by being invisible—not recognizable like celebrities? Are you ever angry that you are not recognized?

9. Culture-Making

As a Hollywood writer, how much do you "create" values, attitudes? If you are uncomfortable with the term "create," would you say that as a writer you interpret or amplify culture, values, or behaviors?

How do you "read" American culture to create a script? What is your understanding of American culture? American values? Attitudes? How much does this understanding influence your work? Do you think you are sensitive to cultural changes? Explain.

What has guided your work? Have you specifically avoided or sought out any topics or special concerns? Does your work contain or try to transmit messages?

What "taboo" topics would you avoid? Is there anything you would not write about? Have you ever "had" to write something distasteful against personal values?

10. Goals

What would the theme of a prize work be?
What would you like to do in the future?
How do you see the future of writers in Hollywood?

Index

163